THE STORY OF WEAPONS AND TACTICS

from Troy to Stalingrad

THE STORY OF WEAPONS AND TACTICS

from Troy to Stalingrad

Tom Wintringham

Coachwhip Publications
Greenville, Ohio

First published 1943
Tom Wintringham, 1898-1949
'Ancient and Modern Artillery,' published March 1855
CoachwhipBooks.com

ISBN 1-61646-541-7
ISBN-13 978-1-61646-541-4

CONTENTS

More than most professions the military is forced to depend on intelligent interpretation of the past for signposts charting the future. Devoid of opportunity, in peace, for self-instruction through actual practice in his profession, the soldier makes maximum use of historical record in assuring the readiness of himself and his command to function efficiently in emergency. The facts derived from historical analysis he applies to conditions of the present and the proximate future, thus developing a synthesis of appropriate method, organisation, and doctrine.

. . . . From the report presented to the Secretary of War at Washington on June 30th, 1935, by General Douglas MacArthur

INTRODUCTION

Two thousand years ago an armoured force was marching on foot towards what is now Sedan; the legions of the first Caesar were moving to the conquest of the Belgae. One thousand years ago an armoured force rode on horses towards the same place, from another direction; some knights who may have owed allegiance to the first King of the Germans, Otto the Great, were settling a little matter arising from the breakup of Charlemagne's almost united Europe. Two years ago an armoured force, speeding in vehicles through Sedan, began the conquest of most of modern Europe. This is one of the patterns that occur in the history of war.

This history of weapons and tactics has been nearly three years in the writing. It was begun when German armoured divisions were storming towards Warsaw—the city from which, about three hundred years earlier, the last heavily armoured chivalry of Europe rode under Sobieski to repel the Turks. It is a book written while the clanging of armour was in all men's ears. It goes through thousands of years of the past to shape our understanding of the Panzer divisions of the present. It starts from the siege of Troy in order to make clear the military meaning of the siege of Stalingrad.

This book has only one aim: that we should understand warfare and therefore win this war. It is not a complete history of weapons and tactics. It is a history of those changes of the past in weapons and tactics that seem to have a bearing on the present, on the revolution in warfare that has taken place in the last twenty-six years, since the first tank ploughed through the mud of the Somme—heading by a freak of history in the general direction of Sedan.

Our need to understand warfare is very urgent today. Many things must be altered. If we are to do the alterations well, we must plan them; that means we must fit them into a general idea of how to fight now and in the future; and that again means we should have a general idea of fighting in the past. If I dared, I would say we must have a theory—the word 'theory' is so much disliked by so many Englishmen, and is considered by them so 'unpractical' that I avoid it all I can; although I cannot see, myself, that it is very 'practical' to do things without knowing the theory of how to do them.

Our difficulty is not mainly in the design, manufacture, and use of our weapons as such. Most of our weapons are more nearly perfect, taken as 'things in themselves,' 'than our enemies'; the difficulty lies in the systems and methods of their use in battle, in tactics, and the design of weapons particularly suitable for use in the tactics now profitable.

Most modern weapons of which I have personal experience seem to me extremely easy to handle after a fashion, and not really hard to handle fairly well. A bullet, I believe, is usually easier to aim at a small target than a football is at a large one. It is certainly easier to aim than an arrow. The business of making a good black pattern on white paper is easier with a machine-gun than with a printing press. As for the mortars and anti-tank guns that modern armies use, they seem far more fool-proof than a vacuum cleaner and much less dangerous (to the man using them) than a motorcycle. I have personally instructed the machine-gunners of three battalions of the International Brigades in Spain in the use of a new type of machine-gun, that neither they nor I had ever seen before, in a few hours of the day before those battalions went over the top; in those few hours the men seemed to get a rough but sufficient idea of the operation of these guns; they were able to work them almost as well as the other types, somewhat worn, to which they were more accustomed. Few soldiers, I think, find great difficulty in weapon training, in learning to use the weapons of today. Even a tank, though tiring, is not very hard to drive. What is hard is to learn where and when to drive tanks, where, when, and in what direction to fire weapons.

It is even more difficult to learn how to combine the effect of a number of weapons, of different types, together with the movement of men who are using or serving these weapons, and of the machines that carry or pull them. The effective combination of fire and movement—soldiers will find it in their training manuals—is the essential problem of tactics. Weapons have no meaning apart from the use of weapons; separated from tactics they become heavy and nobbly things for tired men to carry or drag. It is impossible to learn the right use of weapons without at the same time learning tactics.

Soldiers learn tactics, how to interweave their fire and how to move under enemy fire, by actual experience in training fields and in battle. But they can also learn from reading about the past. No man knows his own trade or profession well unless he knows how people used to do things, not very different in essence from what he is trying to do, under the very different circumstances of past ages. When you are trying to learn to write, you are taught at school how men in the past have written. When you are trying to learn to fight, it is worth while learning something about the tools and machines with which men fought long ago, and their changing ways of using these things.

In any writing of history the writer must choose and arrange the facts described, according to the importance he gives them. I have done this, deliberately, to form an argument. By means of this argument I hope to clear a way towards a theory or doctrine of warfare that is in advance of the Nazi doctrine—more close to reality, more capable of victory.

In other words, I do not hope merely to help the soldier and the junior officer to understand more easily the use of modern weapons, the tactics now taught to him, because he understands those of the past; I also hope that my summary of the changes occurring in them will be of service, in Britain and America, to those who see that victory depends on hard thinking about the art and science of war, as well as on courage and devotion, obedience and initiative.

Some of my general argument about the development of war comes in the first chapter of this book. Its application to modern conditions comes in the last. Some practical friends of mine, including some good soldiers, will ask themselves—or even ask me—why they should wade through the historical chapters between these. My answer is that no one can fully grasp a science or an art unless he gets a clear idea about its history.

Treat fighting simply as a job of work, if you like; it is skilled work and needs learning, like all other jobs from A to Z, from advertising to zoo-keeping. I am sure I could find a complete history of advertising or aeronautics or algebra in any library. But war? A great historian, Oman, wrote a history of the art of war in the Middle Ages. A German soldier, Clausewitz, included a good deal of the history of war, up to Napoleon's time, in his study of it.

We need far more than this. We need—do I not know it!—better history than I or anyone else can write when war presses essential and immediate tasks on all of us. But here is a beginning.

This book is not written only, or even mainly for soldiers. Civilians can neither understand what is happening nor help, politically and militarily, towards victory unless they also have a general idea of war. And war today is a matter for every man's concern. It seizes on all of us; it changes our work, our food, often our place of living, always our way of living. It darkens and destroys our cities; it separates us, in many cases, from our partners in marriage and from our children. A war such as now engages us has, for almost all of us, far more effect and importance than had most wars of the past, wars that were fought far away and scarcely rippled the surface of everyday life for those at home.

There still remain in Britain and America, some who think of war as it used to be, a concern somewhat separate from the life of the nation, a business mainly for those who have chosen the profession of arms, something that cannot be understood by the mass of the people. War seems to these people a matter for the experts. Civilians, and the politicians who represent or misrepresent them should interfere as little as possible with those engaged in the business of fighting. The untrained man, they think, cannot possibly understand even in outline the subtle art of warfare, this mystery to the learning of which experts have to give their best years, their whole lives.

There was a time in England when many of our trades and professions were organised in closed corporations some of which were called guilds. A man entering a profession had to go through a period of apprenticeship that might last for many years. During this period he was supposed to be learning 'the mystery' of printing or of shoemaking.

Our forefathers even made a mystery out of the getting and selling of fish, and one of the most handsome (and doubtless most beneficent) of the greater corporations of the City of London is the Honourable (or Worshipful—the full title escapes me) Company of Fishmongers. The army, in Britain, still retains some of this separate character of the medieval guild. It still wears unusual clothes on ceremonial occasions, or eats its meals with a ritual of which the origin is half forgotten, and its reasons for doing so are much the same as the reasons why the chairman (or Right Whale, or whatever his title is) of the Worshipful Fishmongers will wear on important occasions, at banquets of ceremony, golden chains—chains that are not, as might be imagined, symbols of the hard bondage of the sea, but are more probably symbols of the linked dependence of one man upon another that used to be embodied in the guilds.

To choose a more recent comparison, the British Army often seems very like a collection of those trade unions that flourish mainly in the older trades, in which apprentices becoming 'worthy brothers' go through a complicated rigmarole of customary initiation; as part of this they pledge themselves not to reveal to the uninitiated the inherited secrets of their craft. Sometimes it seems as if, in our army, the skills and weapons of artillerymen or tankmen are carefully not revealed to the ordinary men of the infantry, the uninitiated—particularly carefully not revealed to recruits. And never to civilians.

There was a time when all sciences were secret or half-secret things. Members of the Royal Society, nearly three hundred years ago, peering down the clumsy microscope invented by a fantastic Dutchman (who claimed to see in a drop of water strange tiny creatures not mentioned in the Bible or in Aristotle, and therefore somehow indecent), kept their discussions mainly within their own charmed circle; the vulgar and unlettered could not understand or even be interested in the mysteries that constituted science.

Many things have changed since those days. There are still trade secrets, there are still craft skills. Science still finds its way to ideas that are hard to understand. But any schoolboy with a mechanical turn of mind can read weekly, in journals specially written for him, of all the technique of making and getting and shifting things; an unforgettable film shows us the work of drifters and trawlers, work that was once part of the secret art of a Worshipful Company. And when an Einstein compresses space and time, magnetism and motion, into some new and very difficult formula of relativity, newspapers that boast of two million readers try to explain his theory—mainly in sentences not more than seven words long.

But boys' papers that describe with the most beautiful lucidity the workings of a power station or of a coal pit, when they write of war go in for romantic heroism, of a sort that became slightly old-fashioned in the fourteenth century, or else bewilder the ardent young with nonsense about death rays (and worse nonsense about bomb-sights that make it certain that bombs will hit their targets). As for what the 'adult' press does when it tries to describe and analyse warfare—I had better not give my view on that.

The view that war is a mystery, a secret business, does not suit a democracy. It is absurd that men should be encouraged to educate themselves in ways of getting a living and discouraged from finding out about ways in which they may get their deaths. And when war becomes the principal business of men and women in a population of many millions, they need to have at least a general idea of this business; otherwise their best energies and most vigorous enthusiasms may go adrift in uselessness.

So much of the energy of men and nations has been devoted to warfare in the past three thousand years that even the shortest description of what has happened would fill many books of this size. The thing attempted here is smaller: to describe the main lines of development of the weapons with which men have fought—on land—during most of these years, and some of the reasons why these weapons have changed, and why there have occurred changes in the methods of their use.

This leaves out of account a great many things that have been important in warfare, and are still important. Leadership is important; luck is important; sea-power and sea-fighting are important; and there have been in the past and may again be today beliefs, faiths, and desires, religious and political, that have moved nations to decisive effort in warfare. These things do not come into our picture in this book.

Nor is there any attempt here to make a complete list of every weapon that has been or is being used in war. This is not a catalogue. Too many of the books that describe weapons of the past consist of a simple catalogue hung round with a few stray anecdotes. This is an attempt to explain, not to enumerate.

The omission of naval warfare and naval weapons is not due to a disregard for their importance. It is due to the length of this book and the author's inexperience of war at sea.

I write, then, for civilians and soldiers, being sure that in a democracy at war the part of it that does the fighting and the part that works at home need to have a unity of understanding. They must work together as a team; the civilians must support the services as backs and halfbacks support the forward line in football. They cannot have this understanding without knowledge of past wars. The stevedore deciding how to dump part of a cargo, and the

Prime Minister or President deciding on the aims of whole armies, both need to have a general idea of the sort of war they are waging, the 'priorities' involved, the first things we need to have and to do. So does the sergeant left alone to 'carry on,' his officer wounded or separated from him in the swaying flux of modern battle.

I am not saying that the reading of history and the discussion of theory is the only, or the best, way to learn war. Fighting is the best way. I write before we have invaded Europe, but I hope we shall do so—for many reasons, including the hope that thereby we learn how to fight better than the Nazis, and apply this knowledge to the training and retraining of forces capable of final victory.

Yet whatever fighting lies ahead, and whatever training, the results will be better if our practical soldiers see the need for theory. That is why I labour this point I am English and therefore practical myself. I prefer training or commanding troops to reading up history. In Spain I helped to train several battalions of the International Brigades and a number of officers for those brigades. More recently at the Osterley School for the Home Guard I helped to train five thousand officers and men; at the War Office School, when Osterley was officially taken over, several thousand more. But in this rewarding practical work I found one great lack: the lack of a theory of warfare.

How can you train troops, or command them, if you have no theoretical view of war and its development? Obviously you *can* do it; it is being done. Nothing more than that is being done in most of the British Army. But how do you do it? To judge from my own experience, you do it by having in your mind a lot of ideas about war that are jumbled up together, without order or logic. You do some of the things that everyone else does; you follow the manuals: or you have 'pet ideas' of your own; you 'do your best.' You have some personal experience of past fighting that colours, and perhaps overcolours the picture of war you have in mind. You rely on your imagination—good servant, bad master. And you try to decide by the light of reason between different ideas or 'tips' that come your way.

It is not hard for anyone to see that if you go about the job in this way, the resulting mixture will have a great deal of the past in it. Your own experience, perhaps, of past wars or past campaigns; the manuals' summaries of others' past experiences; the traditional 'we have always done it this way'—these things are likely to dominate what you do. Should they?

I say they should not—unless they are 'rationalised' straightened out by reason. In this book I go driving back into the past, in order to get the past into proper order, in my own mind and in others', and use it for a proper purpose. That purpose is to learn the ways of change. It was, I think, the elder (and greater) von Moltke who used to repeat: 'In war, only change is admissible.'

History ought to tell us how change happens, what are the likely developments today and tomorrow, what 'patterns' are likely to be repeated—like the pattern of armoured soldiers marching, then riding, then driving vehicles towards Sedan, repeated at intervals of a thousand years—or can be made to repeat themselves with changed colours. If this history of mine brings us in any way nearer that understanding, it has been worth doing.

T. W.
London, July, 1942

1
The Theory of the Thing

The battle of Hastings, 1066, is a familiar date to practically everyone. It does not come at the beginning of the history of weapons and tactics—any more than it comes at the beginning of the history of England—but we can start this chapter with it because it provides us with an example of the sort of thing to be explained, if we are to understand warfare. In that year Duke William of Normandy defeated and killed King Harold of England, and achieved the Conquest. Why did it happen? In schoolbook histories, children get the impression that the Norman leader was a better soldier than the English; that the battle of Hastings was won by this leadership, and by the cleverness and the fierce courage of the Normans. All this is, within its limits, true. But something else is left out; and often it is left out of the better histories that are not written simply for school-children; it is, for example, left out of one of the best of these histories, John Richard Green's *The Conquest of England.* A new way of fighting, of handling weapons, of protecting the men who handle weapons—new in England, although it had been developing for hundreds of years in other parts of the world—met and defeated an old way of fighting.

Quite true that William was a better soldier than Harold, though not a braver one. True that the Norman army manoeuvred better than the English, but this was less due to their inborn or acquired cleverness than to the fact that the Norman army had as its shock troops an armoured cavalry; the English fought on foot.

There were reasons for this difference. The two armies' ways of fighting derived, if you go back far enough, from their ways of living, from systems of society or a lack of system or a mixture of systems. And these in turn had embedded in them all the peaceful or warlike history of the peoples that formed the armies. But this connection between ways of living and ways of fighting (between economics and politics on the one hand and warfare on the other) is not the theme of this book. What matters to us is the fact that war was changing, as far back as 1066; a man on a horse could wear heavier armour (and carry heavier weapons) than a man on foot, and therefore the man on horseback—'chivalry'—conquered England.

Armour helped to conquer England then. If England is invaded in the present war, it will be largely with armour that the invaders try to conquer us. The heavy cavalry of the Norman Conquest were the *Panzer* divisions of their day. They had more mobility, tactically, as well as more hitting power than the English infantry they beat. And they had more protection.

Mobility, hitting power, protection—these are, and always have been some of the keys to victory.[1] Where other things—surprise, or concentration at the decisive place and time, or skilful manoeuvre—have won battles, these

[1] These three are, I believe, accepted by British military opinion today, together with morale, as the most important factors in battle. With morale—with which I do not deal here, because this is a book on weapons and tactics—they are stated as such in the best expression of British military thought recently made available, the Lees Knowles Lectures for 1942 by Major-General G. M. Lindsay.

things have usually derived directly from superiority in mobility, hitting power, and protection, or from superiority in one or two of these qualities.

It would be foolish to ask which is the more important of these three qualities. There have been phases of war in which one was all-important and the other two did not matter much. But usually these three qualities have been interlinked in 'new' armies that have altered accepted ways of fighting. That makes the past of warfare difficult to disentangle; it would be far easier if there were only one outstanding factor or quality that always mattered more than others. Then we could analyse the whole past of war according to the development of this single quality.

If mobility were the only thing that mattered, for example, we could split up warfare according to the speed of movement of troops. We should first have foot-slogging war, then horse-riding war, then railway war, then gasoline war. And within these divisions or sections of warfare we could trace developments: the training that made the Roman legions able to outmarch their opponents, the horsemanship of the Saracens or Mongols, the breakdown of the countries with inadequate railroads in the 'railroad war' of 1914-18 (Serbia, Rumania, Russia, Turkey, Bulgaria, Austria), and today the development of the gasoline engine to dominate war. But in fact mobility is not the one thing that matters, always, in all war. And the analysis I have sketched breaks down when you look at the history of war on foot and war on horses.

There has not been a plain and simple progress from marching to riding. Hitting power and protection have complicated this; there have been successive cavalry periods, in each of which cavalry has played a rather different part in the game. There have been other periods when, for reasons connected with hitting power and protection, cavalry has mattered very little.

An attempt has been made to analyse the past of war mainly according to the hitting power of armies, the quality that comes second in my list of three 'keys to victory' (though it might equally well come first). Major-General J. F. C. Fuller has tried it, splitting war into alternating 'shock cycles' and 'projectile cycles.' The reader who wishes to follow this idea from the year 1100 b.c. into the future—to a.d. 2050—will find all these centuries compressed into three pages of General Fuller's book *The Dragon's Teeth* (pages 227-29).

I believe that his division of the periods of warfare (into those in which men fight mainly at close quarters with shock weapons and those in which they fight mainly at long range with missiles and projectiles) is of great value; but it is incomplete and misleading as a guiding thread to the study of all the history of war. This guiding thread ought to show us a pattern that links mobility and protection, as well as fire-power, into a comprehensible shape for the various periods of war. I believe we find it most easily when we start with protection and link with this quality the other two.

Perhaps this seems to me the essential background pattern of war because I am English and have been living and working on this book in an England threatened by invasion. It is natural for me to think of past invasions. England has not often been invaded successfully. The last time it was done, by Dutch William of Orange in the Glorious Revolution of 1688, most of the people of the country welcomed the invaders; it scarcely ranks as a foreign conquest. The foreign conquests that matter in our history are those of Julius Caesar and of Duke William of Normandy.

Caesar led an armoured force to these islands; William led an armoured force; in 1940 and 1941 it was armoured force that threatened us. At intervals of a thousand years or so, these armoured forces, so different and yet in some ways so similar, seem to me wave crests in the history of war. There are other wave crests; but these are the ones that press on my mind in England today.

A primary connection between mobility and protection comes into the pattern. Two thousand years ago it was an armoured force of footmen that bestrode the world; a thousand years ago it was an armoured force of horsemen; today the world reels before an armoured force of vehicles. There are other connections between protection and mobility, but this is the first and simplest. Armour increases until it becomes as heavy as a man can carry in battle, or a horse can carry, or vehicle. Then it becomes overheavy. . . .

The connection between armour protection and hitting power is a little more complicated; before we deal with it, let us attempt a division of the history of war into the periods that are indicated by these armoured wave crests.

First there is a time when men knew little of metal-working, and few men had armour. This prehistory of war need not come into our picture to any great extent, because we know little about it and few clear tendencies are to be seen in that 'dark backward and abysm of time.' This period ends with the battle of Plataea, when the Greek armies cleared the Persians out of Europe. So we get our first period:

I. First unarmoured period—prehistory to 479 b.c.

From Plataea onward the armoured foot-soldier mattered most in warfare until the Roman legion was destroyed at the battle of Adrianople in a.d. 378. That forms the second period in our history of war.

II. First armoured period—479 b.c. to a.d. 378.

Cavalry then became the main arm that won battles; it was usually a fairly light cavalry, not fully armoured. It fought with missiles more than by shock at close quarters. But armour was coming back again, and we can roughly date the return of armour to predominance with Charlemagne's victory at Pavia in 774:

III. Second unarmoured period—378 to 774.

From this time onward the heavy-armoured knight dominated the battlefield. But in the slow-changing Dark Ages and Middle Ages the value of the archer as an auxiliary arm gradually increased, until the Plantagenets found in the Welsh longbow an auxiliary to armour that could master armour. We date the end of this armoured period with the battle of Crécy in 1346.

IV. Second armoured period—774 to 1346.

Our next period has many tendencies within it; it is the whole period of modern warfare up to the point when the tank becomes important. The development of modern industry produces an immense increase in fire-power, and war becomes long-range work in which you scarcely see your enemy. But with the tank, and with the battle of Cambrai in which the tank was first given its chance, armoured protection comes back into the picture. We therefore date this period:

V. Third unarmoured period—1346 to 1917.

And finally we have the present period, in which the armoured vehicle is the dominant arm in land fighting.

We date it:

VI. Third armoured period—1917—?

If we leave out the fringes of the pattern, leave out the prehistoric and the present day, here are solid slices of the past averaging over five hundred years each. Can we find definite tendencies in the development of warfare in each of these periods? Can we find definite tendencies, within each of them, that explain their change into the next period?

Yes. Most of the rest of this book consists of studies of the tendencies within each of these periods. But first it is necessary to define more clearly what I am writing about when I use the words 'tendencies in war.' I am not writing about 'principles of war.' Many attempts have been made to draw up a list of constant, unchanging principles of war. They have all become 'out of date.'

Today if anyone was rash enough to list a body of 'principles,' of unchanging and essential rules of the art of war, his list would probably last a few years, if that. Modern war gathers up into it so many other techniques, depends on and changes so with the changes in those techniques, that it must be thought of as a process which is at the same time continually developing and almost continually being destroyed.

In September, 1939, an important document in the English language listed nine 'principles of war' of which mobility, the power to move, was put ninth. The next year the Nazi Blitzkrieg in the Low Countries and northern France proved that the place of mobility in the list was nearer the top than the bottom. (I think in the next similar list it came second or third!)

So I am not trying to establish 'principles of war.' I know the nine listed; I know other lists of the same sort. They have never helped me much. They may be of more use to others; I doubt it. I am quite certain that some 'principles of war' in the forms in which they are usually taught, are dangerous to the modern soldier. Take, for example, one of the 'principles' laid down in a recent popular book on modern war. The author of this book, who was at one time one of the editors of the United States *Army and Navy Journal,* believes that 'certain scientific principles of war craft . . . are always applicable. . . . They are as unyielding as the laws of mathematics. Just as a college professor and a kindergarten child both will get the wrong answer if they fail to subtract properly, so an army commander and a squad corporal both will court defeat if they fail to protect their flanks.'[2]

This is the 'principle'—always applicable and unyielding—given on the first page of the first chapter of this modern work. A few months after this book was published, the German Army struck in France. Did it 'protect its flanks'?

Since March, 1918, when infiltration was first practiced as the basic tactics of an army, the idea of security by protection of the flanks has been dropped or altered. It no longer governs tactics in the attack. The idea has a limited value, tactically, in defence—a modern defensive position is organised for all-round defence, and has no flanks in the old sense. To talk of flanks in connection with such a position is misleading, because it presupposes the idea of a linear front and a known direction from which enemy forces approach.

Strategically, the question of 'protecting your flanks' is also very different from what it was in 1917. Troops manoeuvring by vehicle (tank, truck, and the like) do not need to protect their flanks against troops shackled to the pace of men marching. Fast-moving troops can carry out

[2] Lowell M. Limpus, *Twentieth Century Warfare* (New York, 1940).

their attacks without fear for their flanks because they go too fast for slow-moving troops to get at those flanks. Later, after the fast-moving troops have broken through, the edges or flanks of the break-through may need to be 'puttied up' with infantry and guns.

Therefore, the words 'protect your flanks' do not now apply to many decisive operations of modern war; when they do to some extent apply to such operations, it is in a new sense, a sense different from that in which the words were used in 1917.

I use this example to show why I reject the idea of unchanging 'principles of war.' But, on the other hand, I repeat that war has tendencies; that these tendencies can be isolated and understood; that the armed forces understanding these tendencies and getting ahead in the application of them will beat the armed forces that ignore or go against these tendencies.

What are these tendencies in briefest outline? They include the pendulum swing between armour and projectile that I have already stated when dividing the history of war into my six periods. They include the general increase in mobility that I have already stated for the armoured periods: foot, horse, motor-driven vehicle. And closely connected with these primary tendencies is the swing of the pendulum between the development of shock weapons for close-quarter fighting and of projectile weapons for long-range fighting. When armour matters a great deal in warfare, shock weapons are normally more important than missile or projectile weapons. Armoured men can get to close grips with their opponents. And the fact that most fighting is done today with projectile weapons does not obliterate this tendency; now that we are back in an armoured period, we still get a change towards close-quarter fighting, and a change towards weapons, such as the tommy-gun and hand-grenade, that are suitable for this form of fighting. Armour and infighting are close companions throughout warfare.

Though there is a swing of the pendulum between shock weapons and projectile weapons, it is usual for one of these forms of weapons to supplement the other. Sometimes one type of weapon is used for one part of fighting and another type is used for another. You can see this almost fundamental pattern of warfare in any group of schoolboys fighting. They begin with stones or shot from catapults, or with snowballs, or with anything they can throw. Then, if the sides are fairly evenly matched and it is a real fight, some of them cease throwing things and come to close quarters with sticks and fists, perhaps with feet. When one side is beaten and scattered, throwing begins again; 'mopping up and pursuit' may continue by 'shock action,' but 'rear-guard actions' are fought mainly with projectiles. In these small schoolboy battles fighting is still the same in essence as it was at various times before the last century. Throwing things, the use of projectiles, is in this form of warfare a useful accessory, but not usually a decisive one. Hitting, at close quarters, among schoolboys, as it used to be very often among soldiers, is the decisive method of fighting.

Later in this history of weapons we shall see how a great change has happened in the past few hundred years, which has led to the use of projectiles becoming the main way of fighting, and has made out of date and useless practically all the weapons by which men used to hack or slice or disembowel each other from a distance of a few feet. These weapons have become relics of the past. The sword, still worn by officers in peacetime and by cavalry, is a decoration and of rather less value on the modern battlefield than the bow and arrow. The spear, which in the ancient world broke empires, and in the Middle Ages was the main weapon of the armoured knight, became in Queen Victoria's time the lance, carried by some cavalry regiments more for the sake of the pretty pennon that fluttered from it than for its use in action. The last important charge by lancers was at Omdurman in 1898. The lance was finally abolished as a weapon in the British Army, by War Office order, in 1928.

The last of these shock weapons, the bayonet, we shall deal with when we come to it. Here we are concerned with the theory of the thing, and this is the important theoretical point already touched on. Even when men fight, as they do today, mainly with projectile weapons, there is still a swing of the pendulum between long-range fighting (such as the artillery battles of 1916-18) and short-range fighting (for example, infantry using hand-grenades against tanks). In 1940 and 1941, shock action was not carried out mainly by shock weapons. Projectile weapons were used—but used at short ranges. Now perhaps the pendulum is swinging back, the range lengthening. This is the sort of thing that study of the past can make comprehensible to us.

The main process of development, during a period when armour and shock weapons matter most, is at first towards the production of an army that can hit like a single heavy hammer. But after a time it is found that such an army is either overloaded with armour and weapons or is too clumsy to be able to manoeuvre successfully against a light and agile foe. So there comes in a second development, by which the army is split up into a number of small units, each under its own separate commander, which are capable of combined manoeuvring. Thus the Roman legion was a much more subdivided organisation than the Greek phalanx which preceded it And with this tendency towards subdivision, there is an accompanying or subsequent increase in the importance of auxiliary arms or units.

During an armoured period, then, we first get simple integration, the making of a solid; then we get complexity coordinated.

During periods of unarmoured warfare, when missiles and projectiles are relatively more important than the weapons used in hand-to-hand fighting, armies tend to depend more and more upon light and mobile troops. There is a tendency away from close order and towards open order. There is a continual tendency towards the production of weapons that can hit your enemy a long way off, before the enemy's own weapons can do you any damage. (This General Fuller has called 'the constant tactical factor.') There is another tendency towards the achievement of rapid fire: if the longbow will fire three times as fast as the crossbow, at the same range, it can be more than three times as useful a weapon. These two tendencies have gone on until modern science and industry have made it possible for each man to carry a weapon with which he has a chance to kill any enemy he can see; modern weapons, in the shape of long-range artillery, will also kill at a greater distance than it is possible for the men handling them to see; and some modern weapons can be fired ten times a second.

These fairly simple patterns of the development of warfare become complicated by others. There are the questions of fortifications and of transport. When great cities grew up, men learned a lot about building. And this made possible the development of fortifications; there are periods in warfare when the arts of fortifications developed so far that they influenced tactics much more than the arts of metal-working and weapon-making. And people moving to and from the cities, and goods being brought to them, made roads necessary and wheeled transport. The development of roads, with the occurrence of periods of history in which good roads were allowed to fall into decay, has always affected tactics to a very great extent. Wheeled transport has often dominated supply, and therefore the size and mobility of armies. Today it does more than that.

The size of an army never depended on a simple decision by a king or emperor: 'We will have another hundred thousand soldiers.' The size of an army depends first on the agriculture and the general level of production in the country concerned. How big an army can be brought to battle is often limited by the food and other supplies it needs and by the stores and supply (transport) services available.

These political and economic factors or patterns in war I put down here, for the purposes of my argument, as 'complicating factors.' Some, like those I have mentioned, arise from the obvious connection between the technique of a society—its civilian skills, wealth, knowledge, trade, industry, and agriculture—and the fighting forces that are in part developed or conditioned by all these economic factors. Others arise from the moral or political growth of societies.

War is sometimes spoken of or written of as mainly a matter of heroism and ideals, of courage and service. These certainly occur in warfare and often become more noticeable during war than they are in peaceful civilian life—though it is worth remembering that courage is usually useless against much better weapons. Yet even for courage there is often a 'sensible' reason. The history of a country and its geographical position sometimes make some of the war aims of that country essential to its life and growth. If these war aims fully penetrate the people of that country, and are deeply felt by them, the soldiers who represent that people in battle will be different from, and better than, soldiers who know nothing about what they are fighting for and have no national interest in the outcome of the struggle. In the same way, men who feel themselves free, and able in some way to take part in the decision whether there shall be war or shall be peace, put more of themselves into any fighting that comes their way because they feel that it is something they have themselves helped to decide, a responsibility they have chosen. In this and other ways the politics or class structure of a society affects the morale of its soldiers, and therefore their tactics.

Another similar factor has a direct influence on tactics. As men develop new tools and new weapons, new ways of living and of fighting, each war and even each battle can be of a slightly different shape from those preceding it. There are some forms of society that change very little. Asiatic monarchies, ruled by a king or emperor who is supposed to be descended from some god or other, are usually organised on the lines that nothing ought to change; all old customs are good; everything ought to be done just as it always has been done in the past. And more progressive nations sometimes take a breathing spell, when customs and past ways of doing things are preserved by conservatism. When societies of this sort go to war, their generals and other soldiers have an out-of-date idea of what war is like. They do not alter their tactics to make full use of the new weapons that science and industry have made available. They have a reactionary or conservative theory of warfare, or they have no theory of warfare whatever and just carry on by habit according to regulations laid down long before. Such societies produce armies that are usually destroyed by the armies of nations which are more ready to adopt new methods, more ready to face changes and to learn quickly the use of new things.

Because many people nowadays believe you can measure strength in battle by simply counting the numbers of tanks or divisions available, it is worth emphasising that questions of technique, of weapons and tactics, have often been much more important in war than the relative size or productive wealth of the countries concerned, or the numbers of the populations involved. A great master of the art of war said that 'God is on the side of the big battalions.' But the remarkable thing about warfare through thirty centuries is how often the big battalions have been defeated, in spite of that advantage, by forces very much smaller. It is only when war falls into a rut, and the armies contending fail to mobilise the forces making for change and progress within their own nations, that battles become a simple matter of counting the heads on each side. Then, in that stagnant and unskilled sort of war, you secure victory because you still have a few men left when mutual slaughter has killed off or exhausted enough of the men opposed to you.

I have chosen to treat many of the ways in which warfare is affected by economics and politics as complicating factors for a simple reason: I want to isolate from the extremely complex business of battle a small number of tendencies that I believe to be inherent in the nature of war itself. They seem to me tendencies that are part of the very stuff of warfare and to govern the other complicating factors, using or rejecting them. Take, for example, the tendency that General Fuller calls 'the constant tactical factor': the tendency already mentioned to produce weapons that kill at longer ranges. It is a tendency that is natural to war, inherent within it. (I agree with General Fuller that it is important, though I am certain there are other tendencies of equal importance that marry with it or conflict with it.) This drive towards the production and use of weapons that will kill your enemy while he is a long way off, 'before he can get at you,' governs and employs much of the civilian skills of a nation preparing for war. Today it produces long-range bombers. Two thousand or more years ago it produced longer spears than the world had seen before. Whatever the state of a society or its level of technique, this is a 'constant.' And yet men in battle today are often at closer grips with their opponents, fight at shorter ranges than they did twenty-five years ago. This is a paradox that can only be resolved when we see that other 'constant tactical factors' exist, which interact with that mentioned—for example, the tendency already mentioned to increase armour up to the maximum that can be carried effectively, or even beyond that maximum.

The tendencies inherent in warfare usually take soldiers by surprise; as these tendencies develop, they take on the horrid appearance of 'dastard tricks' of the enemy that no one had thought of, tricks or techniques that cannot be resisted. Superior civilians sometimes condemn soldiers as wooden-headed because of this; but actually foresight is usually difficult for them because war, in so far as it is a science at all, is a special sort of science in which experiments can seldom be repeated with any exactitude, and in which the discovery of reliable principles for planning and action is unusually difficult. Compare it, for example, with engineering.

The science of engineering changes because new materials are discovered and new processes. The engineers' products become more powerful or more speedy or more economical, cheaper to make or giving better results; and although there may be pauses in this process there is a fairly continuous line of advance. At the same time many of the fundamental things known about engineering do not change. There are constants. The principle of the lever remains unchanged, although better levers are developed to replace those more primitive. The principle that we were taught at school to call the 'law of conservation of energy' applies to the most modern Diesel engine as it applied to the first steam engine. Each invention or alteration in technique is built up on a pyramid of proved and tested facts discovered in the past. This is a science. War is only in part a science; it contains few constants.

There are thousands of years of warfare which are governed by simple propositions, such as the proposition that men drilled to cooperate will beat an equal number of men not accustomed to cooperating, or men armoured will beat an equal number of men unarmoured, or men with weapons that can reach a long way will beat an equal number of men with weapons that reach a short way. But always these propositions are complicated, in each separate and 'real' battle, by questions of leadership and morale, by the weariness or the energy of soldiers, the food and rest that these men have had, by accidents of weather and of the countryside. The engineer who has designed and tested an aeroplane motor can watch it wear out in the certainty that he will learn some of its weak points, and then make a better engine; the commander going into an important battle may have no second chance and can have no effective rehearsal that includes all the facts known and unknown to him. He can move pins or make pencil marks over maps; he can play his war game or train his troops in manoeuvres; but the actual test of battle comes to him each time as an unknown grouping of dangers and opportunities. In his orders there may be clear principles that he believes he is following, but these principles later seem to the impartial observer only very rough approximations to reality. Battle is unrehearsed—even unprincipled. It is, in this sense, an art, and a particularly difficult art.

A group of dancers will practise their ballet in conditions very similar to the conditions under which they will perform; an army practises war under conditions necessarily unreal. The German Army at one time is said to have practised at manoeuvres with blank cartridges in which there were a small number of live loaded cartridges, so that real bullets occasionally whistled by, and the army was given a fairly close approach to reality at a small cost in casualties. I have seen the same thing done usefully at a British school of battle drill. The war dances of certain primitive tribes are also on occasion dangerous and good practice. But most armies practise battle in conditions very different from those in which they must perform; because of this, war is one of the most unstable of the arts. You can rely on dancers or singers to reproduce in their performances, night after night, very nearly the same level of excellence; armies only 'do their stuff' at intervals, always in unrehearsed positions and usually at unexpected moments.

It is precisely because war is not continuous that war is difficult to understand or to develop logically. (This is not an argument that war should be continuous.) During the intervals between wars there is no effective measuring-stick for old weapons and tactics or for new. Industry has a measuring-stick, in profit or production; medicine has one in the death-rate or the numbers of cases of illness. A soldier in peace has no such guide; and it has seldom been suggested to him that he should take as his aim the full employment in warfare of all the civilian skills and resources and developments of his nation in peace. This brings us to the final point to be made in this chapter.

I have tried to trace some of the tendencies, inherent in war itself, that govern all warfare and divide its history into a number of periods, within which changes different in scale but comparable in type have occurred. Next, I have tried to outline these tendencies within each type of period, armoured or unarmoured. Now I must try to state the causes for the changes from one period to another, the causes for the big breaks or discontinuities or emotions in the history of war. The first of these causes inherent in the nature of war itself, is the one we have just been stating: the difficulty of judging during peace the probable shape of the next war.

I have already pointed out that conservative societies base their ideas of how to fight on the past and ignore the threads of change. Armies have been in the past, in most societies, some of the most conservative elements in those societies—and this is natural for the reasons I have been labouring. Old ways of war—become old. They are successful for a long time; in particular the almost invulnerable armoured man is successful, until it seems he always will be successful. Then the break, the change, comes partly because he has been so successful that he has not felt the need to alter, to keep up with the times, to do new things. That is how old ways of war lose; but how do new ways win? Where are the living roots of the revolutionary sort of change in weapons and tactics which is different in quality from the gradual developments occurring within each of the periods of war?

I believe that the positive roots of this sort of change lie outside the normal development of warfare. Changes of this sort are not in their essence technical developments inherent within war; they arise more from the complicating factors of economics and politics than from war as a separate science. The change from an armoured to an unarmoured period, or in the reverse direction, occurs normally when the peoples who make up a nation, or several nations, discover for themselves new forms of social organisation or in some other way release new popular energies.

This sort of change, producing a new way of war, often comes because a people express themselves in a democratic or popular or revolutionary way; it always comes because of civilian or non-professional intervention in warfare; it does not come from armies separated by their profession from the rest of the nation. These propositions are challenges. To myself, writing as the armies of Fascism, which have swallowed up and in a sense become the Fascist States, are still 'on top,' these propositions are also hopes.

2
Some Talk of Alexander

It is not of great importance for us to study the first unarmoured period in warfare, or to attempt to trace tendencies and developments in that period. In this chapter, therefore, we simply note the principal characteristics of the period and then go on to the first armoured period, which begins with the defeat of the armies of the Great King of Persia by the fully armoured citizens of Greek city-states.

The weapons of the first soldiers were of course the weapons with which men had hunted wild beasts for thousands of years. In the hunting of wild beasts, for food or safety or sport, men learned to cooperate in groups; and these groups, when men were hunting men, became the first armies or units of armies. Weapons changed slowly; arrows tipped with flakes of flint, such as had been used by cavemen of the farthest past against wolves and deer, were still employed by 'native levies' that formed part of the Persian army invading Greece in 480 b.c. Other troops in this army had wooden javelins with fire-hardened points. Others carried slings with which they threw missiles of about the weight of a baseball (five and a quarter ounces). (One army of an earlier date mentioned in the Bible, had seven hundred slingers out of twenty-seven thousand men; they 'could sling stones at a hairbreadth, and not miss.'

For some reason—possibly because they carried swords in their right hands—these Biblical slingers were left-handed.) There were better-armed troops in the Persian army of 480 b.c.; the soldiers that we have mentioned were from the more backward parts of the world conquered by the Persians, but their weapons show what all weapons must have been like in the far past before there was any written history.

The armies of this far past must have consisted mainly of light troops; they were not drilled or ordered; they fought like mobs or herds. And they fought mainly with projectiles. If they came to grips hand-to-hand, the normal weapons would probably be stone axes or wooden clubs, for in those days men did not know how to handle metals and therefore could not make any effective stabbing instrument. Even when they first had some metals, they could not sharpen them as blades; they used tomahawks, or similar weapons.

Huntsmen and soldiers, in the far past, were always looking for the best sort of rock with which to tip their arrows and throwing-spears. We shall never know who first discovered how to pound up metal-bearing rock and heat it in the fire until the metal melted and could be shaped. But we do know that, quite naturally, the first metals with which men worked and from which they made weapons, tools, and ornaments were the softer metals—gold, silver, copper, and the like. Of these, gold and silver are too soft for anything but ornament and coins (though royal troops in some Asiatic monarchies had decorative spears tipped with silver or gold). But from bronze you can make fairly sharp points for arrows and spears and cutting-blades for short swords. The blades have to be rather short and thick; they blunt easily and bend fairly easily; it is impossible to make a full-length sword from bronze. About the period when the mists of the past are clearing a little, and we get the first stories and poems that are the beginnings of history, we find that the more progressive peoples are fighting their wars with bronze weapons. And they are beginning to wear bronze armour.

Any sort of metal armour, even if it is made of soft metal, will protect the wearer against light or blunt projectiles that are not travelling very fast. So as far back as the Siege of Troy, perhaps a thousand years before Christ, the fully armoured man seems to have been able to advance in spite of most of the projectiles he was likely to meet; he could, if he chose, come to hand-to-hand fighting with his opponent. An army at this time consisted of a relatively small number of great men who possessed this rare and costly full equipment of armour and a very much larger number of lightly armed hangers-on whose arrows and throwing-spears were still the main weapons; their tactics still dominated the battlefield. Because the fully armed men were so few, they often fought in single combat; but at this period they seldom seem to have moved in groups that had any definite formation to them—though there is a description in Homer's *Iliad* of a line of men standing in order 'like a wall.'

A typical battle of this period, if we are to believe Homer (who, although, or because, he was a poet, was also a very vivid war correspondent), begins with the armies forming rough lines opposite each other. A Trojan leader 'shakes his two spears in the air' and challenges some Greek to come and fight him; he 'dares the bravest of the Grecian race.'

One of the Greeks takes up this challenge; the Trojan has a fit of nerves and tries to get lost within his own army; but his brother jeers at him, he recovers his nerve, and after an immense amount of palavering it is decided that these two shall settle the whole battle by single combat. They then toss up to decide who shall first throw a spear at the other. After the spears have been thrown and the Trojan champion has been well beaten, another Trojan picks up a bow, made of two goats' horns joined together, aims at the Greek champion, and wings him. Other Trojans, disappointed because their champion has had the worst of it, 'rush tumultuous to war.' So the fighting becomes general; each of the leaders gathers his men; chariots are driven round at speed (one of the Greek leaders tells his charioteers that if one of them gets tipped out of his chariot he should 'mount the next'). But most of the officers mentioned in the subsequent casualty lists are those wounded or killed by spears thrown at them with such force that they penetrate shield or helmet. Arrows account for a few of the killed and wounded, and there are some cases in which men are injured by big rocks thrown at them. The number of those hurt in close hand-to-hand fighting is very small.

The chariots in this case are not often used for shock action; they are simply mobile platforms from which the soldier throws his spear or from which he dismounts in order to do some real fighting. In other parts of the world, at the period before real history begins, chariots are mentioned as the favourite battle units of the armies of the greater kings (with, usually, cavalry as the other main force in these armies). The Israelites, fleeing out of Egypt, are not afraid of King Pharaoh's archers or spears-men, but of his chariots and his horsemen. And hundreds of years later, when 'the Assyrians came down like a wolf on the fold,' it was their chariots that impressed the chronicler. It seems certain that at a fairly early period the chariot began to be used as a shock weapon; it was driven straight at the opposing army and was intended to smash through that army, knocking down or running over any man who was in the way. It was much more useful for this purpose than the cavalry of the period. The horseman, having then only a primitive saddle and no bit in the horse's mouth and no stirrups, could not control his horse well enough to make a real charge possible. A horse carrying a rider who has not much control over him will swerve away from the enemy ranks at the last moment of the charge. But the charioteer, bracing himself against the wall of the chariot and hauling on the long reins (connected to a bridle if there is no bit), is able to control his horses by main force and overcome their fear of the obstacle in front of them.

Chariots at all times remain special weapons of opportunity—weapons that can be used rarely, only effective at the right place and moment. Because horses are large targets and can be put out of action by a few arrows, chariots cannot be left standing under enemy fire. And because chariots need very smooth ground over which to operate, they have always been weapons more suitable to the desert and the plains than to warfare in broken country. When men had learned a good deal about the use and tempering of the harder metals, it became customary to lash scythe blades to the wheels and axles of the chariots.

A Roman poet, Lucretius, describes these arms in a most terrifying way:

> They lop off limbs so instantaneously that what has been cut off is seen to quiver on the ground before any pain is felt. One man perceives not that the wheels and devouring scythes have carried off among the horses' feet his left arm, shield and all; another, while he presses forward, sees not that his right arm has dropped from him; a third tries to get up from the ground after he has lost a leg, while the toes of the dying foot quiver on the ground near by.[1]

[1] Lucretius, *De Rerum Naturae,* III, 650-62.

But, although this poet makes it sound as if the wild chariot was an impossible thing for the ordinary soldier to meet successfully, his countrymen of the legions usually despised them as tricky and unsatisfactory weapons, too dependent on ground to be of much solid value. The Roman legionaries did not often think it worth while to take chariots into action and usually kept them for triumphal processions.

The main business of battle, many hundreds of years after the Siege of Troy, was still in the stage that is dominated by projectiles and to a lesser extent by cavalry and chariots. As iron and bronze became more common and men more skilled in working these metals, it became possible for small armies to be fully equipped with armour so effective that few projectiles could penetrate it, and with solid metal-tipped spears that an unarmoured cavalry could not face. It was impossible to equip the enormous armies of the Asiatic despotisms with this complete kit of armour; only the officers could be properly protected. But before 500 b.c. most of the citizens of Greek cities possessed the full equipment of the Hoplites, the Greek heavy infantry. This equipment included a large helmet covering the back of the neck, and sometimes the cheeks and chin, as well as the top of the head. Most of the Greek helmets were plumed, and the plumes of horsehair or some other stiff material made the soldiers look tall and frightening—an idea that still persists in the busbies and plumed hats assumed by modern soldiers when forced to wear the fancy dress called full uniform.

The Hoplite wore a heavy breastplate and backplate of metal, joined at the sides and shaped to fit him. These plates were made of one piece and must have been extraordinarily uncomfortable and exhausting in a hot climate. It seems to have been normal for a Greek soldier to be accompanied by a slave who carried his armour and helped him into it when action became necessary. From the waist, or just below it, to the knee was not armoured; from the knee to the ankle the Greeks wore what we might call shin-guards; they called them greaves. And each soldier carried on his left arm a large shield, usually round, with which he tried to catch the point of any arrow or spear that was. coming his way.

A soldier so equipped could stand up to most of the projectile weapons that were then known, and could usually keep on advancing until he got within striking distance with his spear. The normal Greek spear was, in 500 b.c., a shaft some eight feet long, made of ash or some other hard wood, and tipped with iron. And the Greek armies which several times defeated much larger Persian forces about this period did so mainly by their ability to close with and kill, by spear and short sword, their much more lightly protected enemies.

The Greeks' armour was only one factor in their success. Other factors derive, not from the economics of Greek life, but from its politics. Two of the things that free men delight in—and the Greeks were free men as compared with their opponents—are dancing and gymnastics. The Greeks developed both of these much further than other peoples. They therefore acquired the habit of controlled movement in close order, which is the essence of drill. One historian describing the decisive battle of Plataea (479 b.c.) suggests that the Persians must have looked with amazement on the Athenian and Spartan infantry moving down hill to attack them, and must have thought that these strange Greeks were carrying out some new sort of war dance. For each Greek soldier moved in exact line with his neighbour, all their shields on the same level so that they formed an unbroken wall. To do this effectively the Greeks had of course to keep in step; keeping in step was something that the Persian armies, made up of all sorts of subject peoples and only roughly lined up by officers with whips, had never attempted and perhaps had never seen.

The third factor that made the Greeks immensely better soldiers than most of the Persian army was their morale. There is sometimes held to be an antagonism between the freedom of the individual and efficiency in warfare. Throughout history, governments that were concerned to hide their own inefficiencies or double-dealing have insisted that the citizen ought to sacrifice his freedom to know and to argue, for the sake of unity in war. Actually the Greeks and others of their time proved conclusively that this freedom is part of the moral equipment of a people desiring success in war, so that from their time onward it began to be recognised that slaves are relatively useless in warfare, and that even tyrannical organisations of society need to foster, for the purposes of warfare, a class of citizens who feel themselves to be free. The maintenance of such a class was part of the policy of the Roman Empire during its years of strength, as it had been of the Roman Republic before it.

The morale of the Greek soldiers, based on and developed by their relative freedom, gave them the necessary courage to advance to hand-to-hand fighting. Any schoolboy who has taken part in some sort of gang battle will realise that it does not require so much courage to throw things, and dodge things that are thrown at you, as it does to dive right into the scrimmage and start using fists and elbows. In the same way men needed to be specially courageous at this period in warfare for them to fight as the Greeks did.

The Greek way of fighting was new; it was therefore condemned by many advanced professional soldiers of the day as being very barbaric and primitive; a Persian general, used to cavalry and chariots and the swift movement of light troops, is known to history for his words of scorn for the Greeks' artless, slogging massacres—and for the subsequent massacre of his own troops by these barbarian methods.

The Greeks had developed their normal shock tactics in the warfare between their own cities. These cities were usually walled and too strong to take. But a city could be starved out by the army of another city if the hostile army occupied the fairly small patches of very fertile land that provided the first city with food. Therefore, a Greek army could not stay for very long behind fortifications; it had to come out and meet the force that was ravaging its fields.

While there were a large number of sieges in the Greek wars of the fifth century before Christ, these were seldom prolonged for more than one campaigning season. But in 413 b.c. an Athenian army was sent to besiege Syracuse, a city in Sicily that had been originally a Greek colony. In this long siege, of great importance to Athens and to its allies and enemies in Greece, the Athenians were not dealing with a normal small city that would starve if its fields were ravaged. Syracuse was an immense trading centre, with allies and tributaries in many parts of Sicily and trading stations in many ports; and it drew much of its food from across the water. It had large stores and warehouses. The Athenian attempt to ravage the countryside, on which they wasted nearly a year, failed to reduce Syracuse to starvation because supplies could be brought in from other parts of Sicily and from farther abroad. Therefore, the Athenians attempted to cut off the city from supplies by building at wall behind it which would shut it in on the land side, while their navy blockaded it at sea. This was one of the first essays in large-scale position warfare (warfare based on fortifications that are not the walls of a city) of which we know much. The Greeks must, however, have had some experience of this form of warfare; as far back as the Siege of Troy they had built fortifications of a sort to protect their ships; later the Athenians, whose city is separated from the sea by several miles, had built two long walls of fortifications joining the city and its port, so that when Athens was besieged, supplies could come in by water.

It was probably this siege of Syracuse, at which the Athenians were defeated just before they finished the wall with which they intended to blockade the city, that led to the first development of artillery—of a sort. Dionysius, the Tyrant of Syracuse, is known to have possessed, a few years after the siege, a considerable number of wooden machines called *ballistae* and *catapults*. The *ballistae* threw light stones a certain distance in a fairly straight line. The catapults lobbed heavier stones up in the air, throwing them a shorter distance. When, very much later, another Dionysius invented a machine that would fire arrows one after another in rapid succession, the ancient world had its equivalents of the field gun, the mortar or howitzer and the machine-gun.

These machines, made of wood, will be described later. They soon became the dominant weapons in position warfare, in the sieges of cities and the defence of walls. But their influence on mobile warfare was slight. Like the chariots, they were weapons of opportunity that needed smooth ground. They could not travel as fast as cavalry or chariots, or even as fast as a well-trained infantry. They could seldom be integrated into ordinary war.

Such long-range weapons were introduced from Syracuse into Greece about the middle of the fourth century before Christ, and were greeted with the usual lamentations that are caused by new weapons. The Spartan leader Archidemus groaned, when he first saw a catapult drop a lump of rock on a man standing some way off, 'O Hercules, the valour of man is at an end!' But in fact warfare in the open field went on very much as it had always done, and valour was still a necessary (though sometimes an overrated) military quality.

The most usual formation of a Greek army in the fourth century before Christ consisted of a simple line of spearsmen massed about eight deep. The Greek shield was often between three and four feet in diameter, and it seems probable that this line of spearsmen would march in very close order, so that one man's shield tended to protect to some extent the man to the left of him. There was a tendency of Greek armies to edge towards the right as they moved down to battle, because the shield was always carried on the left arm and it was natural to advance this arm and shoulder. If you walk with your left arm and shoulder forward, you are apt to swing to the right, a bit. There was also a natural tendency to dislike being outflanked on the right, because that was your relatively unprotected side, the side you could not cover easily with your shield. But in the early Greek armies there was not much sign of the ability to manoeuvre. Tactics scarcely existed; you lined up, charged at the run, fought hand-to-hand until you had made your enemy run, and then looked round to see if there was any more fighting to be done somewhere else. The only subdivision of the average Greek army was that each city contained a number of tribes; these usually fought together under their own leadership.

The Spartans, the best soldiers in Greece, had a more logical and useful subdivision of their armies into units like our battalions and companies, so many men to each. As the Greeks learned more of warfare, they evolved one fairly simple (but very useful) tactical idea: to hold or 'fix' your enemy with one portion of your force, and then attack him from an unexpected angle with another. But they did not specialise their troops or weapons for this fixing and hitting.

Here, then, is our 'first armoured period' fully formed. What of the tendencies within it?

The first tendency was towards concentration of force to acquire a temporary local superiority at some part of the battlefield. Such a concentration had occurred before by accident, or by a general's choice of his line of attack. Now for the first time it was planned, organised before the battle started. Epaminondas, the first general to see that an army must as a rule—not as an exception—be stronger in one part than another, invented the phalanx.

The phalanx was, at first, a wing or division of the army that was ranged sixteen deep instead of eight deep. Because it was so much heavier than the eight-deep line opposed to it, the phalanx could usually penetrate the enemy line and therefore throw it into disorder. We shall see the idea of the phalanx coming into warfare at intervals from the days of the armoured foot-soldier to those of the armoured vehicle.

Epaminondas also exploited another tactical device. His main striking force, the phalanx, was usually placed on one wing of his army; the other wing was 'refused.' It was held back from the first stages of action, either by being aligned at an angle away from the enemy or by moving into action more slowly than the phalanx. This weaker wing of the army did not meet the enemy forces opposed to it until those forces had been disarrayed by the impact of the phalanx farther along the line. This manoeuvre, planned before action, is very similar to the 'oblique order' with which Frederick the Great won many of his battles. And it has its parallel today in the *Blitz* offensive on a narrow front, the attack on a wider front not occurring until the enemy's positions have been pierced.

In the north of Greece there came to the throne of Macedon a remarkable king, Philip, who carried the shock tactics of the Greeks to their logical conclusion. He formed all his heavy troops sixteen deep, made all of them a phalanx, so that if they met an ordinary Greek army the weight of their mass could smash through the Greek line. And he equipped these men with immense pikes, something altogether solider as well as longer than the spears of the Greeks. The *sarissa,* as this pike was called, was not a throwing-spear converted into a shock weapon, as the Greek spear was. The *sarissa* was twenty-four feet long, and was so carried that eighteen feet of its length stuck out in front of the soldier. The heavy butt behind him helped to balance it, but must have made it very difficult for him to turn or manoeuvre.

King Philip of Macedon trained his soldiers to move in very close order, each man only two feet from the man in front of him. Five of the pikes of the men behind the first rank appeared in front of the first-rank man. The other ten spearsmen, massed behind, could not at first use their spears, which they carried slanting upward. But as soon as a gap appeared in the front ranks of the Macedonian army, through casualties or the sway of battle, there were plenty more spears to fill this gap and maintain an unbroken frontage of six spears to each width of shield. The bristling mass of this Macedonian phalanx could bear down any opposition that it met; it soon made the Macedonian kingdom the dominant power in Greece.

Here is the first tendency in the 'armoured period'; the army like a heavy hammer—simple integration. The next tendency, towards coordinated complexity, treads on its heels.

Philip saw that this heavy 'hedgehog' of an army he had invented was a bit clumsy, even for the steady foot-to-foot slamming of a normal Greek battle. He therefore split up his army, making each large unit a separate phalanx and leaving gaps between these units. In order that the flanks of the units should not be too vulnerable, they were sloped back so that spears and shields were at a slanting angle rather than in a straight line across the front. Sometimes each phalanx was wedge-shaped.

Philip's brilliant son, young Alexander, divided this heavy infantry into brigades, and subdivided these into regiments and companies. He trained his men so that each company, eight deep, could wheel to a flank or face-about, which is no easy job when men carrying twenty-four-foot pikes are massed together. Or two or three companies could be massed behind each other. Normally each regiment marched into action separately, but the gaps between the regiments were filled by lighter troops whose business it was to protect their flanks from cavalry or chariots. These lighter troops could keep position when crossing rough patches of country, which the heavy armed men of the phalanx usually had to march round. When it became possible to close up the phalanx or its brigades for a charge, or when there was a heavy attack by cavalry, these lighter troops would usually be withdrawn to the rear or given space within the protecting walls of the heavy companies.

Alexander added to his heavy troops archers, slingers, and javelin men, and a certain amount of cavalry. His heavy cavalry were armoured and their horses were also protected; this cavalry carried long lances and heavy swords. His lighter cavalry were mainly bowmen and were used as skirmishers.

Alexander also carried with him to battle a certain number of light catapults and used them as a sort of field artillery. Unusual in his willingness to accept new ideas, he made of his army a testing ground for every sort of weapon that was known to his age and combined all of them with the heavy troops which were the main force on which he relied. There are few soldiers in the ages following Alexander's of whom as much could be written.

Here, then, are the auxiliary arms appearing fully, to support the armoured phalanx. It was with an army of forty-seven thousand men, made up of the elements described, that Alexander met the Persian King Darius at Arbela in 331 b.c. Although accounts of the size of Asiatic armies have often to be taken with a grain of salt, it seems clear that the army of Darius was not far from being a million strong. If the size of the Persian army is taken as that of this page, the size of Alexander's army would be equivalent to only about one and a half lines of print.

The Persian forces were not only much stronger numerically, they also possessed two special weapons. One was the chariot with scythes on its wheels; the other was a formation of fifteen elephants. Elephants had not previously been used in warfare outside India, and it is probable that very few of the Greek army had ever seen such animals. They must have seemed as terrifying to Alexander's men as the first British tanks did to the German soldiers of 1916. But they proved of very little use in battle. Elephants are wise animals that like to live several hundreds of years. They therefore avoid unpleasant and noisy situations, and are likely to stampede during a battle. Why should they face a line of soldiers glittering with spears and armour and yelling loudly? It is not clear what happened to the elephants at Arbela, except that they were badly scared. (On another occasion, hundreds of years later, when elephants were used during Hannibal's last great battle, many of the beasts stampeded when they heard the Roman trumpets. They destroyed the order of Hannibal's own African cavalry, making it possible for the weaker Roman cavalry to chase it off the field.)

At Arbela the Persian king had drawn up his immense army at one side of a wide area that had been carefully cleared of rocks and other obstacles. The Persian idea was that they could use this levelled space for the chariots. After a day spent on reconnaissance Alexander moved his army in oblique order diagonally towards the Persian left flank. This movement was so directed that the bulk of his forces were likely to get beyond the levelled space, on which the chariots could operate, before they made contact with the Persian flank. The Persian king was therefore forced to send forward first his cavalry and then his chariots into action considerably ahead of his main line, where they could not be supported by the rest of his troops.

The chariots might have done a great deal of damage to the heavy phalanx if they had been able to attack the Macedonian spearsmen without meeting any other opposition. But as soon as they came rattling over the levelled plain, Alexander's lieutenants sent forward lightly armed troops, at the run, to oppose them. These poured their arrows on the horses and charioteers, dodged the chariots and ran alongside them, slashing at traces and even seizing reins. Few of the chariots got through this mosquito cloud of light troops, and fewer still were under much control. Then, as the chariots came to the phalanx, each brigade packed a little more solidly together and opened, between itself and the next brigade, lanes down which the terrified horses could bolt. Some of the chariots went right through the Macedonia infantry without damaging it, and were captured by Alexander's cavalry far in the rear.

Such a battle must have been, for the most part, a mixed and whirling affair of cavalry charges, the disordered open fighting of the light troops, the uncontrollable dash of the chariots, the panic of the elephants. There were scarcely more tactics in all this than in the scrambles round Troy. But there was one element of order and precision that was the basic thing in Alexander's strength: the massed power of the phalanx. It could not have succeeded alone; and it is possible that the majority of the Persian casualties were caused by the spears of the Greek cavalry, not by the spears of the phalanx. But it was the irresistible march of five brigades of the phalanx, turning inward towards the level ground and the Persian centre as soon as the chariots had spent their force, that broke the Persian line and also broke the nerve of the Persian commander.

For many generations after Arbela the phalanx was unbeatable. But there are few Alexanders in the world and many men who think that drill and discipline are the sole foundation of soldiering. In their hands the phalanx became once again a solid body, homogeneous, the parade-ground general's ideal, but not easy to manoeuvre, not subdivided into separate units, and not combined with other troops in Alexander's way.

Alexander's successors, who split up his empire between them, tried to make soldiers of inferior quality, even slaves, carry out the tactics of the phalanx. But these soldiers had neither the tradition nor the morale of the Macedonians, and they could only act as clumsy 'hedgehogs' of spearsmen, without mutual support and without the power to combine with other arms. The combination of separate and different arms, even at this early period, was becoming an essential thing in tactics. When it was a simple (or stupid) combination, the units merely added to each other; when it was Alexander's sort of combination, the power of each arm multiplied the power of the others.

Occasionally during this period a phalanx of spearsmen met another phalanx in battle. In this case victory usually went to the luckier side or to the side that had the more solid soldiers in the more rigid formation. War swung back temporarily from the flexible combinations of Alexander towards the formation of armies that were heavy and clumsy hammers.

But in a campaign carried out by the Macedonians in Italy, the phalanx met its master. The tough farmers of central Italy, who had gained experience during a series of wars against their neighbors and against invading Gauls, had produced a rather different method of fighting. They used almost the same weight of armour as the Macedonian heavy troops and a more effective shield, but they trained their men to manoeuvre rapidly in small units, in such a way that they could come in on the flank of any solid body of spearsmen that opposed them or split up any charge of horsemen. They relied more upon short swords than upon long spears, because long spears cannot be manoeuvred quickly in a new direction. Their first ranks also used heavy throwing-spears. The Roman legions were forming.

At first the Macedonian phalanx, if it held together, could usually drive these Romans off the smoother portions of a battlefield; the lighter Roman formations and shorter spears could not oppose the long *sarissa* handled by a compact mass of armoured men. But the phalanx could not pursue the Romans or split up their flexible small units, or even drive them out of rougher country, woods, or hillsides. And after the phalanx had been in action for a time, some of those forming it were wounded by the throwing-spears of the Romans, or wearied by the weight of their own great pikes, and they lost cohesion a little. Then the Romans jumped in with their swords, much handier weapons than the pikes for a 'mix-up.' So King Pyrrhus of Macedonia won a number of victories over the Romans, but each victory cost him more than he gained by it. Since that time any costly and futile victory in war has been known as 'a Pyrrhic victory.'

The Roman legions, when fully formed, were 'heavy troops'; they fought in close order; their shields could be locked together to cover them against projectiles. They relied increasingly on throwing-spears. This combination of shock tactics with short-range projectile weapons gave the Romans a great advantage. They combined the order and discipline of the Greek phalanx with a superior 'fire-power.' The spear (*pilum*) could not be thrown far; but it could wound an enemy spearsman before he could get close enough to use even the longest of pikes.

The Roman spear was heavy because more than half its length consisted of iron. The iron point was integral with an iron shaft over four feet long. Inside this shaft, driven well into it, was a four-foot handle of wood. The whole length was six to seven feet.

Against cavalry and light troops this weapon could be used as an ordinary spear. Against a solid infantry it was thrown. Gradually, as the legions found it necessary 'to hit before the other fellow could' and therefore needed a longer range for their 'projectile,' they lightened and shortened the *pilum;* the iron shaft became three foot long, or less, and the wooden shaft was also shortened.

The Roman infantry normally fought in three lines, one behind the other, each line eight deep. At first only the front line had throwing-spears, and the second and third lines a longer thrusting-spear—a remnant of the old Greek phalanx. Later the first two lines had throwing-spears, then all three lines. The lines were not often continuous: the usual formation was like three lines of black squares on a chessboard, with white squares empty between them; and the units could be even more widely spaced.

A legion of six thousand men was divided into ten cohorts, and each cohort had three 'maniples,' one in the front line, one in the second, and one in the third. It was therefore, 'extended in depth'; as reinforcements came from the rear lines, they were men of the same unit as those they were supporting, accustomed to the same officers. This, and the open nature of the chessboard pattern, which allowed movement of the reserve units to a flank or allowed them to fill the gaps in the front line, gave the Roman commander full control over his men. He could spread them to outflank, or concentrate them to break through, the enemy's line. Even Alexander's brigades, regiments and companies were clumsy compared with the Roman legions and their cohorts and maniples.

When a Roman army was robbed of this flexibility, given it by its open formation, it lost much of its fighting strength. Its leaders, therefore, had to be careful of their flanks, because flank attacks on a Roman army could squeeze it too tightly together, and the cohorts would then lose their power to manoeuvre. The usual battle order of a Roman army included a force of cavalry on either flank, whose duty it was to hold off enemy flank attacks at least until the legions had got to close grips with the main body of their opponents.

At Cannae the Romans were defeated by Hannibal in a battle that ever since has been the budding general's dream. Hannibal's army was scarcely four-fifths the strength of the Romans'; his special weapons—elephants brought with infinite difficulty through Spain, southern France, and across the Alps—were not particularly effective. But his cavalry was powerful. In his order of battle his centre (infantry) was pushed forward. As the Roman legions advanced to the attack, this centre gave ground slowly. The middle of the line gave more than the wings. This refusal to meet in a decisive clash gave the Carthaginian cavalry on the flanks time to drive the weaker Roman cavalry units off the field. Then Hannibal's lighter troops, which had mingled with or followed the Carthaginian cavalry on each flank, turned inward and caught the Roman infantry from each flank. The Roman legions, which had been moving forward into a narrower and narrower space as the enemy's centre retired, were pressed closely together; they could no longer manoeuvre; the men who had used up their throwing-spears could not get new ones or be replaced by others with new ones. The front ranks began to be filled with wounded and weary men, who could not get to the rear because of the unbroken, close-packed lines behind them. Then Hannibal's victorious cavalry took them from the rear. The net closed, in a swaying mass the Romans were butchered, until nothing that could be called an army remained.

The Romans learned from that battle the tactic of 'envelopment.' From that time onward it was the normal desire of every good Roman general (as it is today of every German general—how many times the German communiqués in this war have contained the triumphant word *zuzammenpressen,* squeezing, to describe successful envelopment!) to carry out a *Cannae*—a double envelopment of the enemy's flanks. And the Romans learned many other war tricks from the Carthaginian people whose wits had been sharpened by trading and the sea.

The strength of the Roman legion was greatly increased, during the 'world war' of Rome against Carthage, when the Romans conquered Spain and there developed a new weapon. Spanish iron ore provided at that time, and from that time until modern days, has provided the best metal in the world for the making of weapons. The quality of the metal and the skill of the men who tempered it made it possible for the Spanish sword to be sharper, more pointed, and yet lighter than the weapon previously carried by the Romans and by other soldiers of the period. It was not a long rapier such as that used by fencers today; it was shorter than the swords used by many other troops of the period; but its ability to pierce through the joints of armour, and its handiness due to light weight and good balance, made it the dominant weapon in hand-to-hand fighting for a long time. And it did not blunt or bend easily; most swords of the period were good only for half a dozen hard blows; the Spanish sword was good for years of fighting. This Spanish sword was introduced into the Roman Army by Scipio

Africanus, the general who achieved the defeat of Carthage.

Carthage was a trading empire. Its power was in its wealth, its ships, its possession of protected harbours throughout a large part of the Mediterranean. It had no considerable class of free citizens from which it could form its armies; most of its free citizens manned its navy. It found, as was always found in the ancient world, that slaves made poor soldiers. In Carthage, therefore, there developed, probably for the first time in the world, a large-scale mercenary army; most of Hannibal's soldiers fought for pay—not as men forced to fight by national or local compulsion, and not as volunteers whose main motive was to defend or extend the power of their own country.

The mercenaries who followed Hannibal were far freer men than those who were tied by law or custom to follow some ruler or form part of some army. This freedom gave them part of their ingenuity, their craft in war. They were dangerous enemies.

In the social organisation of the Roman Republic there remained at first much of the primitive patriarchal organisation of society. Only the head of the family could own property; all the young men were supposed to be entirely subject to the orders of the oldest man in the family. But faced by the Carthaginian Army and suffering from its ingenuity and power to manoeuvre, the Romans had to depart from this old and hampering social system, which crushed the initiative of its young men and gave them no incentive to act for themselves. The Roman soldier—then always at first a citizen—began to be permitted, by custom and then by law, to possess a separate form of property, called the *peculium castrense,* the possessions in the camp. This was the first legal form in which the right of individuals (other than fathers of families) to moveable property was recognised.

In this way the Roman legion became a body of free citizens with special rights of their own which were in advance of the rights of civilians of the same age. The legionary became economically as free an individual as any in the Roman world. With the pride in himself that came from this freedom, and with the morale of the well-fed, patriotic peasant or artisan, he beat the Carthaginians.

He became then, or later, as Rome conquered wider fields, a long-term professional soldier. During his years of service he was subjected to the hard and difficult drilling that is necessary for shock tactics; he was trained to march farther and faster than any army had marched before him; and he carried on the march a heavier load than any tackled by soldiers until 1915 or 1916. Sometimes he had baggage wagons, but often he had to move hundreds of miles with this load on his back. The armour and the weapons were heavy enough; each man had to carry in addition a supply of food and two or more large stakes from which the outer wall of a camp could be constructed. Discipline, marching and carrying power, depend enormously on morale. The legionary's morale was civic—'civis Romanus sum': I am a citizen of Rome. His fighting strength, therefore, depended largely on his position as a free citizen of the world's greatest city. The eagles of the legion bore the letters S.P.Q.R.: 'the Senate and the people of Rome.' When the legions ceased to consist mainly of such men, they were on their way down hill.

In the next chapter we study the end of this armoured period, the breaking of the legion. But here, looking back from today—when the men of the Panzer divisions and the Russian, American, and British tank forces have not only a special power but a special pride as the *élite* of the armies—we can look back to the Roman legions and understand them and yet marvel at their achievements. The legion was not always undefeated; it sometimes suffered serious defeat when used by inefficient leaders, or without the necessary cavalry to protect its flanks, or against a more mobile enemy or in unsuitable country. The armies of Rome once had the misfortune to be led by a man who had made his way to power in Rome principally by his wealth; and this man, Crassus, took the legions to utter defeat at the hands of Scythian cavalry who used scarcely any weapon but the bow. These bowmen never fought pitched battles, but harried the marching legions for hundreds of miles across the half-desert spaces into which Crassus unwisely led them. There is a limit to which any army can go against the guerrilla; and the Roman legions found that limit in the deep forests of Germany as well as in the bare uplands of Persia. But these were wars at the edges of the known world; throughout the area that was then civilisation (or our civilisation, for in this book I have to leave out China, separated from our world by deserts and by mountains) the Roman sword and throwing-spear and armour were almost unconquerable. From the century before the beginning of the Christian era right up to the fourth century after, the soldiers who imposed the peace of Rome upon most of the known world were the solid, hard-marching, heavily armoured footmen, the legionaries.

3
Knights Were Bold

Between the two great wave crests of armoured warfare of the past, between Caesar's legions pressing across the English Channel and the knights of Richard Coeur de Lion turning their pennons towards the Holy Land, lie many centuries of change in war. The first of these changes is the breakdown of the Roman legion, the ending of our first armoured period. Then comes the second unarmoured period, the great days of light cavalry. Later again comes a heavy armoured cavalry to rule the world in the new shape of feudalism. These three changes are the subject of this chapter.

Behind the breaking of the Roman legion there were, of course, political changes extraneous to war, but usually expressing themselves through war. Somewhere, far off among the nomads of the steppes in Central Asia and Siberia, changes of climate or growth of population or the merging of tribes into nations produced a raiding pressure on the 'barbarians' who lived along the frontiers of the Roman Empire. These restless barbarian tribes and nations kept up a heavy pressure on those frontiers from about a.d. 235. And at the same time within the Roman Empire the concentration of uncontrolled power, and other causes, led to continual civil war, In the sixty years after a.d. 235, sixteen emperors of Rome and thirty would-be emperors were assassinated or fell in battle. The citizens were no longer numerous enough to form all the armies needed; 'barbarians' had to be taken into the legions. The legions fought among themselves, against their emperors and to change their emperors. A wild tribe or nation, the Goths, broke through the solid armoured crust of legions and reached the centre of the Empire, where there were few reserves; these Goths ravaged whole provinces. Provinces rose against Rome, or the Eastern Empire fought the West. To meet the strain of almost continuous warfare, the legions were pulled to pieces and lost their sense of pride and solidarity as units; one cohort would be in Britain, another in Germany, another might have been snapped up for a march on Rome by some general who saw the chance to become Caesar.

And with these changes on the political field went others of a more military sort. The small garrisons along the frontier, thin-spread and without enough reserves behind them, came to rely on auxiliary weapons and arms more than had ever been the case before. For their own defence they relied more on artillery, 'engines' throwing arrows or great stones, and for attack on raiding barbarians they began to rely more and more on cavalry, because of its mobility.

Out of the experience of countless raids and scuffles and of pitched battles between legions, it became clear that artillery was far more dangerous to an armoured infantry marching slowly in close order than it was to cavalry riding fast in more open formations. This reliance on artillery for defence, therefore, increased the tendency towards the use of cavalry for the attack.

The legion lost in mobility to some extent by taking with it, into the field or to its temporary camps, the artillery from its main garrison positions. It could no longer march swiftly enough to catch raiding parties of Goths or Germans or Vikings.

There was no longer a clear distinction between the free citizen of Rome and the men of the conquered provinces; increasing numbers of the latter came into the legions and into the auxiliary forces. These auxiliaries grew in number. Units of the Imperial Guard, most of them light infantry or cavalry, multiplied and were considered more important troops than the legion.

The 'barbarian' volunteers or mercenaries in the Roman Army, whether enrolled in the legions or employed as cavalry and light troops, were no worse soldiers in battle than the Roman legionaries had been. The legend that they were not so courageous or so skilled—is a legend. But they followed their paymaster; or they went with any usurper who could promise them a chance of success, of loot, of power. They had no longer the citizen's sense of a Roman community and a Roman peace that made the legions of the Republic and the early Empire relatively proof against the temptations of Caesarism. And they were no longer opposed mainly, as the earlier legions had been, to forces less well organised and armed than their own. They were mainly opposed, in the civil wars, to other legions like their own, armed with weapons exactly like theirs. That is why they gradually gave up the heavy *pilum*, which, although thrown, was as near a shock weapon as any projectile could be, and adopted a lighter throwing-spear to get more range, 'to hit the other fellow first.' This change weakened their power to deal with heavy attacks, and particularly with a determined cavalry charge, which had usually been met by the legion using the *pilum* as if it were a pike. The lighter spear could range farther, but was no pike; it was useless except for throwing.

Meanwhile, the possible enemies of the Romans became stronger. In the early days of Rome, when Tacitus first described the Germans, they were 'without helmet or armour, with weak shields of wickerwork, and armed only with the javelin.' In other words, they were still in a primitive projectile stage of warfare, undisciplined and unable to fight with shock weapons. But after three hundred years of contact with the Roman Empire they had learned much. Thousands of their men had served as Roman mercenaries. They had traded across the frontiers, and in exchange for furs or amber they had received iron and armour. Most of their rank and file, at the time when they began to break down frontiers of the Roman Empire, had heavy shields bound with iron and a long cutting-sword that gave them more reach than the Romans had. (Metals had improved and become more plentiful; but the Roman sword seems to have been the same in a.d, 300 as in 200 b.c.) Some of the Germans had developed a deadly weapon that they handled with particular skill, the *francisca,* a heavy battle-axe or metal tomahawk which, whether swung or thrown, would split the Roman shield and go through Roman armour. Dangerous though these Germans were, the superior discipline and control of the legions could keep them in check until the whole Roman way of fighting was destroyed by the Gothic cavalry at Adrianople in a.d. 378.

Here for the first time cavalry became the shock troops that mattered. Battles had been won by cavalry before, used in combination with other arms; battles had not before been decided primarily by cavalry. The Goths, big men on big horses, armed with heavy lances, swept the Roman infantry into a huddled mass where men were so crowded that they stifled and no man could lift his arm to strike a blow. When the emperor, with all his chief officers and forty thousand of his men, lay dead on this battlefield, the day of the legion had at last ended and the day of the man on horseback had begun. And for nearly a thousand years from that day the man on horseback ruled warfare.

What were the root causes of this great change in war? We saw in the last chapter that the change to the armoured footman came with the Greeks, who all wore armour and fought as solid masses partly because they were all citizens on an equal footing. The idea of equality, under king or law or aristocracy or representative, that governed the politics of the Greek cities, governed also their military technique. They were perhaps the first well-drilled armies because they were also the first armies of fairly free men. That is not so much of a paradox as it may sound today: men do things better and more easily by their own choice than they do under compulsion. From these qualities of the Greeks came the first 'break' in war; did the second, the 'break' away from armour, come from the same sort of cause?

Yes, the roots of this change were of the same sort, though naturally they were not identical. The decay of Rome, the growth of Caesarism, made the Empire brittle. Outside its strained defences milled the barbarians, ruled by the rough, primitive, unorganised, semi-democracy of tribe and clan. These barbarians learned from Rome. But they did not learn to form legions of their own, to become an armoured, drilled, and close-knit infantry. They learned how to make the qualities of their own societies tell in war. They learned how to become a raiding and charging cavalry, which, although unarmoured or lightly armoured, could beat shock troops by shock tactics. And besides their shock tactics they had the missile weapons we have already described.

Soon these missile, weapons became all-important.

Sir Charles Oman, in his *History of the Art of War in the Middle Ages,* describes the process: 'The day of the sword and pilum had given place to the day of the lance and bow.' He quotes Vegetius' *De re Militare,* in which that admirer of the legion deplores the abandonment of armour: 'so our soldiery went out with breast and head uncovered to meet the Goths; and perished beneath their missiles. . . . For what can the footman armed with the bow, without helm or breastplate, and even unable to manage shield and bow at once, expect to do?'[1]

Oman continues:

> It is of course ludicrous to suppose that, at a time when the cavalry were clothing themselves in more complete armour, the infantry were discarding it from mere sloth and feebleness. The real fact was that the ancient army of mailed legionaries had been tried in the battlefield and found wanting. . . . Roman military men had turned their attention to the greater use of missile weapons for the foot-soldiery, and to developing the numbers and efficiency of their own cavalry.[2]

Within this period, the second unarmoured period, there was a tendency towards the development of a completely mobile cavalry consisting almost entirely of archers. The Huns under Attila became so feared that their name lingers still in Europe as a symbol of ruthless war; they were a people of horsemen who could pour out a rain of arrows as they rode. Belisarius, the great general who held together the Empire of Byzantium, ascribed his victories over the Goths to the fact that 'our own Regular Roman horse and our Hunnish Foederati [allies] are all capital horse-bowmen, while the enemy has hardly any knowledge whatever of archery. For the Gothic knights use lance and sword alone, while their bowmen on foot are always drawn up to the rear under cover of the heavy squadrons. . . .'[3]

[1] *A History of the Art of War in the Middle Ages*, pages 8 and 18.

[2] *Ibid.*, page 19.

[3] *Ibid.*, page 32.

The horse-archer, whose missile was the dominant weapon of the period, often wore armour of a sort, and his opponent, wielding a shock weapon, the lance, also wore some armour. But this protection was usually light and incomplete. In the case of the first Turkish armies to clash with the soldiers of Byzantium, armour was almost entirely lacking: 'The Turkish hordes consisted of innumerable bands of light horsemen who carried javelin and scimitar, but relied not at all on their armour for victory.'[4]

Mention of the Turks has already taken us up to or beyond the period when war changes again, the second unarmoured period. And here it is necessary to stress that dates are very arbitrary things; ways of fighting do not change, throughout the whole world, in the same year. When at Plataea the armoured Greeks destroyed the army of the Great King, there was not an immediate end to all the old ways of fighting, or everywhere a beginning of the new. In the same way there was no complete and immediate reversal of tactics and change in weapons in the year of the battle of Adrianople, a.d. 378. The change in this case, in the parts of Europe and Asia that were then the 'civilised world,' took about two centuries, from a.d. 250 to a.d. 450. In other parts of the world—perhaps in fact as 'civilised' or more—such as China, the changes described may have happened at other times, or not have happened at all.

But the main thing I am trying to trace is the development of weapons and tactics in Europe and Asia that leads in direct succession to modern war. And here we have to note that during the second unarmoured period the tendency around the centre of civilisation was largely towards an army made of horse-archers, or towards one in which

[4] *Ibid.*, page 204.

the horse-archers played a dominant part. This tendency reached its fullest development (by a sort of time-lag, an overlapping) long after a new armoured way of fighting had begun to develop fully in Western Europe.

The army, made up of horse-archers, reached its fullest development with the Mongols, the armies of Genghiz Khan. Modern American commentators have seen in the tactics and strategy of Genghiz Khan a parallel to the *Blitzkrieg* of the Nazis. There is the same use of treachery and fifth-columnists, the same surprise and suddenness in attack, the same strategy of penetration and encirclement, the same sort of mobility. But there the resemblance ends. The tactics of the *Blitzkrieg* are largely tactics of heavy armoured troops fighting at shorter ranges than those normal in an earlier sort of war. The tactics of the Mongols were those of very light cavalry, fighting at the maximum range possible with the missile weapons of their day.

Before the Mongols appeared from Asia, war had swung back to armour again in Western Europe. If armour is strong enough, the horsemen wearing it can charge through the arrows and get to close grips with their enemies. As early as a.d 451, the army of the Huns under Attila had been checked and turned back at Châlons by the shock tactics of a heavier cavalry. In a.d. 732, the light horsemen of the Moors, who seldom wore armour, invading France from Spain, were defeated at the battle of Tours by an infantry armed with the sword and by a heavy cavalry, fairly well armoured, which fought mainly with the spear. In each case it seems possible that the invading armies had tired their horses before action. These armies rode animals suitable for the plains of southern Russia or the spaces of North Africa, but not heavy enough for the soft fields and tracks of France.

This latter victory encouraged the Franks in their development of armour. Soon a great leader arose among them, most of whose first laws dealt urgently with the question of the accumulation of armour and its 'economical' use. Charlemagne, King of the Franks, forbade all merchants to export armour from the territory he ruled. The heavy penalties enforced show the eagerness with which men sought this key to success in war. In a.d. 814 a chronicler described Charlemagne and his army riding into northern Italy:

> Then appeared the iron king, crowned with his iron helm, with sleeves of iron mail on his arms, his broad breast protected by an iron byrnie, an iron lance in his left hand, his right hand free to grasp his unconquered sword. His thighs were guarded with iron mail. . . . And his legs, like those of all his host, were protected by iron greaves. His shield was plain iron, without device or colour. And round him and before and behind him rode all his men, armed as nearly like him as they could fashion themselves; so iron filled the field and the ways, and the sun's rays were in every quarter reflected from iron. 'Iron, iron everywhere,' cried in dismay the terrified citizens of Pavia.[5]

Probably this chronicler was exaggerating. With Charlemagne, the second armoured period is fully begun. But not all of Charlemagne's cavalry can have worn a complete kit of armour. It is unlikely that any except the best-equipped of his men had a metal covering to the neck; they would have a metal cap and a thick leather covering

[5] Oman, *op. cit.,* page 86.

over ears and neck. This was the first form of the knight's headdress, the hauberk. But soon (that is to say by the next century) the material hanging from the metal cap or 'tin hat' was fine chain mail, iron links interwoven, and this was brought forward to cover the chin and the neck. The lower edge was tucked under or tied over the mail shirt or 'byrnie.' This had originally been as short as an ordinary waistcoat today; it later became as long as a pullover. And then these two pieces of armour were made into one garment. The mailed shirt acquired a hood of mail which was pulled up over the 'tin hat,' and covered everything except a small space through which the horseman could look out and breathe.

Although Charlemagne's men cannot have been so well armoured as later knights were, we can take the date of his battle at Pavia (a.d. 814) as marking the beginning of the second armoured period.

In the tenth century the better-armed men began to wear a strong iron bar connected to the helmet and sloping down in front of the nose. This was to guard against blows at the face that would turn aside from the helmet; it probably lasted for over two hundred years, until the great days of knighthood when the helmet with visor covered the whole of the head and face. In the visor, which could be lifted from in front of the eyes and mouth when the knight was not fighting, there were small holes through which he could see and breathe. This type of helmet is that best known to most people who have seen medieval armour either in museums or in pictures.

In Charlemagne's day the average armoured soldier seldom had protection for his thighs. But a hundred years later the mailed shirt was usually lengthened till it reached the calves. It was, of course, divided to make riding possible. Breeches of mail, which must have been torture to ride in, were not used until much later.

The round shield had almost disappeared. It was still carried by Danes and by some other foot-soldiers. But for the man on horseback it is inconvenient to have a large shield, since the left hand must be used for the reins when the right hand is using lance or sword. A very small round shield, carried, as a rider must carry it, strapped above the elbow of the left arm, only covers a part of his body that is already protected by his mail shirt; it does not cover the more vulnerable lower parts which, on a horseman may be exposed to spear-thrust and sword-slash from the ground. The shield of the early Middle Ages was therefore shaped like the commonest form of kite that children fly; the long lower end could be carried to cover the left knee or set across the saddle.

While armour increased in this way, until its weight came near the limit that a strong horse could carry, weapons altered less. Danes and Franks, as infantry, used a double-handed axe, sometimes also double-headed, to cleave through armour. The sword grew longer; but in the early period of the Middle Ages the horseman's lance was seldom a long and heavy weapon; at Hastings the Norman knights sometimes threw their lances as well as thrusting with them. Men were still learning to make good saddles and stirrups; without these a heavy lance is dangerous—if the knight sticks such a lance well into his opponent, the horse goes on, but the victorious knight slides off over his beast's tail.

The armour of the Franks was too stout to be pierced easily by the ordinary arrow. And thanks to this armour Charlemagne achieved something that the Romans could never achieve, and no subsequent ruler—save for a short time Napoleon and Hitler—could so much as attempt. He united in one state France and Germany. When that unified state fell to pieces at his death, the wars of modern Europe were beginning to take shape.

At the battle of Hastings, which we can take as a convenient point where the early development of feudalism is shown in its completeness, the English represented the more primitive, 'backward' form of warfare of the period, lacking most of this feudal development. They were foot-soldiers; they were lightly armed; their weapons were swords, javelins, clubs, axes, and a few short bows. They fought in a solid mass, six or twelve deep, behind a low ditch and a stockade of brushwood and hurdles, roughly put together and covered by shields. Behind their shield wall the English crouched for protection from the Norman arrows, standing up to throw their axes or other hand projectiles when the Norman cavalry came near.

The Norman army was a very different organisation. It did not consist, as the English army did, of men raised by a primitive 'conscription,' under which every family owning so many acres of land must send to war one man with infantry equipment, or, if they owned less, a man with some primitive weapon. Duke William of Normandy brought with him most of the barons from that province, and a large number of feudal adventurers seeking, 'some for land and some for pence.' Their equipment was that of the foremost knighthood of their day.

His army, however, did not consist only of heavy cavalry. The first line of each of his divisions consisted of archers with a smaller number of crossbowmen; the second was made up of his foot-soldiers—younger sons, knights' squires, poverty-stricken adventurers—most of whom wore mail shirts, unlike the bulk of the English infantry, who came straight from the plough in the leather jerkins they normally wore.

Behind his secondary troops came William's main force, the armoured knighthood.

William opened the battle with his bowmen, to whom the English could scarcely reply. But when these archers came forward within range of the English hand-thrown axes and javelins, they got too heavy a shower of these and broke back to the protection of the Norman infantry, moving forward with spear and sword. This infantry drove back, to the breastwork, some of the English who had been running a little way down the hill to get close enough to fling their missiles at the archers. But against the main line of the English infantry, the Norman infantry—much outnumbered—could not make an impression. They were probably already retreating a little from the missiles thrown at them, and from the English pikes, when William's horsemen came up the slope as hard as they could ride. At many points these horsemen must have swept down the English hurdles; but they could not push through the stubborn English infantry, whose axes cut through shield and mail, felling horses and lopping off limbs. After a fierce medley, William's centre and right wing fell back a little, to regain its order; his left wing fled down the hill.

Whether or not this flight was a deliberate manoeuvre, it led directly to the defeat of the English. They had been tormented by arrows to which they could give little answer; they had met and checked easily the Norman infantry. Now, after heavy hand-to-hand fighting, the English on the western end of the battlefield saw their opponents riding away downhill in panic retreat; saw these horsemen clumsily break into and sweep away the units of Norman infantry that had rallied behind their advance. It was natural for this primitive English army, with no considerable leader save its king to control it, to dash in pursuit after the beaten enemy.

But William was not beaten. He had rallied and reformed his centre. He saw to his left the English pouring downhill, having lost formation and lost the protection of their stockade and their shield wall. William turned his horsemen and crashed into them as they moved. His heavy horsemen were no longer riding uphill, but along the slope of the hill parallel to the crest. His opponents were no longer stubborn ranks twelve deep, but a scattered line of men tunning across his front. When Duke William had finished this charge, nearly a third of the English army was cut to pieces.

The remaining two-thirds had not moved. William ordered a second general attack, in which the breastwork was probably destroyed entirely and the shallow ditch filled up with the bodies of men and horses. This second assault fared better than the first; the two brothers of the English king were killed and the English suffered severe loss. But their long line of shields and axes still held the hill crest.

Now William showed the value of the mounted soldiers' mobility, power to manoeuvre. He ordered a large portion of his command to wheel about and pretend to fly. The English thought, again, that their enemy was broken, and again a large body swept forward from the English line. Again William charged to the flank, and again his cavalry rode over the scattered English ploughmen.

The centre of King Harold's army, his own personal forces, better armed and more solidly controlled than the levies of the English shires, still held their ground. They continued to fight for some hours, under conditions steadily becoming more desperate. William's cavalry roved round the compact mass into which the English line had settled. William combined a series of charges, which kept the English pressed close together, with flights of arrows that could not miss their target. After some hours of this unrelenting pressure, the English ranks were filled with wounded men who could not press to the rear because of the close-packed mass of their comrades behind them. The English had no more javelins or axes to throw, no weapon with which they could reply to the bitter arrows. 'A strange manner of battle,' says a chronicler, 'where the one side works by constant motion and ceaseless charges, while the other can but endure passively as it stands fixed to the sod. The Norman arrow and sword worked on: in the English ranks the only movement was the dropping of the dead: the living stood motionless.'[6]

In spite of this merciless harrying, the English held till evening. Then as a last resort William ordered his archers to fire their arrows high in the air so that they fell from above on the English, some of whom must have been too weary to lift their shields above their heads, some of whom may have been too closely packed together to do this. One of these arrows wounded King Harold mortally; a last charge of the Normans broke through to the king's standards and cut them down.

The battle was won; but even after the winning, the English took some revenge. The slope behind the crest on which they had been standing was very steep; many of William's knights charged down it in pursuit of the scattering English and came to grief at a small brook with sharp banks below. It was nearly dark, and neither horse nor armoured man could keep his feet. Turning back, a remnant of the English caught these knights scrambling with their heavy gear along this brook and killed them at close quarters. This savage counter-attack, which the Normans thought must have been delivered by fresh English reinforcements, nearly caused a panic among the victors. One of William's chief subordinates urged him to retreat before these new forces of the enemy. But Duke William was a better soldier than that; he rallied his cavalry and

[6] William of Poictiers, quoted from Oman's *History of the Art of War in the Middle Ages.*

moved it forward along safer slopes. The English, almost all their leaders killed, and perhaps two-thirds of their army, slipped away into the woods.

The armoured cavalry that won the day at Hastings and dominated European warfare for a long period before and after that battle was seldom used in such a way that its *strategic* mobility was of importance. Its job was not to ride round the opposing army and outflank it, nor to move swiftly upon some outlying section of it and deal a decisive blow before this detachment could be reinforced. The art of war knew little, at this time, of 'fixing and hitting,' or of envelopment. The main job of the medieval knighthood was to act as shock troops, breaking into and riding down the mass of the opposing army.

At the same time it possessed a capacity for *tactical* manoeuvre which was greater than that of any infantry force. William's charges to the flank, by which he caught and destroyed the sections of the English army that rashly left their stockade, are examples of this mobility.

The heavy cavalry, the dominant arm, was used alone or almost alone by some of the less progressive commanders of the period. The use of archers to disturb and harass the array of an opposing army, and the use of infantry to hold positions, to clear difficult bits of country where the knights could not easily make progress, to prepare the way for knights in assault, and to form a solid rallying-point for them if their charge failed—the use of these auxiliaries in proper combination with the heavy cavalry became the highest level of feudal generalship. William the First, in his handling of his archers, and particularly in his use of high angle fire against a tight-packed target, showed exceptional realisation of the value of combining auxiliary arms with his principal formation. The history of feudal war is full of the failure to achieve such a combination; over and over again during the Crusades the knights of

Western Europe were defeated because their leaders relied too exclusively on the men on horseback. But there were few cases when the man on foot was more than an auxiliary—useful, perhaps indispensable, but not the main force in battle.

In feudal society, in its classic form, all land except that held by the Church—and even some of the property of the Church—was supposed to be held from the king. The king, in return for his grant of land, was entitled to ask from the men to whom he granted it various forms of service, including military service. If the estate was a large one, the service would not only be that of the man to whom it was granted, or some individual of that family, but would be the service of retainers and tenants who in turn were bound by feudal law and custom to act as soldiers, either for a customary period or when required, under their lord.

Feudal society arose because of the need for some security, authority, protection, during the centuries of raiding and looting that followed the breakdown of the Roman peace. To any community exposed to the raids of Vikings or Vandals there was little protection to be gained from any far-off emperor; the strong walls of a local lord's castle were their best shelter, and his power to raise a local force their only hope of successful action against the raider. It was natural that such a society, based on these needs, should concentrate most of the available weapons and armour in the hands of the lord whose social function it became to give some measure of security to 'his' people.

The first thing that the lord saw to was that he himself and his men-at-arms were fully equipped; this was a necessity, not only for the protection, but also for the governing, of his area. He was a professional; his sport or profession was warfare. Other people scarcely needed arms, except for the few who accompanied him to battle.

This order of society was particularly suited to the production of relatively small armies consisting of very heavily armoured cavalry. And this 'chivalry' was for a time almost invulnerable to most of the normal weapons of foot-soldiers.

A lasting memorial of this feudal civilisation consists of its castles. But with the development of these, and of the machines used against them, we can deal in a later chapter.

Though we have taken the conquest of Britain by this armoured cavalry as an example convenient for our history, it achieved other and greater conquests. While the Normans were winning for themselves baronies in England, the chivalry of Castille was winning Spain back from the Moors. The Moors and Turks and Saracens remained in the older, previous way of war: they were mainly lightly armoured horsemen fighting with missile weapons. That is why the armoured chivalry of Europe was able to clear Spain and to invade Africa and Asia during the Crusades.

But the second armoured period, like the first, had within it the seeds of its own destruction. In our account of Hastings we have mentioned the value of the archer to the shock troops, the cavalry. It was the development of this auxiliary that gave the knight his deathblow, in a change that was also the ending of feudalism and the beginning of the modern world.

4
Yeomen Bowmen

'So the knights in the first French battle fell, slain or sore stricken, almost without seeing the men who slew them.'

In these words a chronicler described the fate of armoured knights at the hands of English and Welsh archers in the battle of Crécy, in 1346, that ends our second armoured period. We are entering the time when men are killed by those whom they cannot see, the modern age of long-range fighting, which contains so much of the modern world that it must fill several of our chapters.

The bow and arrow had been known for many thousands of years; they come into the first battles of which we know anything. The change that made the bow, from an auxiliary, the main weapon in warfare during the second unarmoured period has already been described. It was retained as a principal armament by the Asiatic 'horde' armies that persisted in that unarmoured way of war and never achieved the armoured knighthood of Western Europe. But in Western Europe it disappeared for a time because almost useless against good armour. Instead of it the crossbow was developed.

The Romans of the period of the legions had possessed a weapon very like the crossbow, but had never considered it very important. They seem to have left it in the hands of light troops and auxiliaries. It perhaps should be considered the most mobile form of the 'artillery' with which the Romans equipped themselves towards the end of the period of the legions. Then in the Dark Ages it seems to have been forgotten.

In the second unarmoured period in Western Europe and in Asia it was not used; this was a period of the horse-archer, and the crossbow was too heavy and clumsy for a cavalryman to use. Somewhere in the tenth or eleventh century the idea of a small 'hand-machine' that could be used by a single foot-soldier was revived. It could fire a heavier projectile, of some use against armour; that is probably why it reappeared at this time.

The crossbow consisted essentially of two short arms of wood and a stock roughly shaped; the arms were much stiffer and stronger than those of an ordinary bow, and could only be pulled back for a few inches by a man hauling on the cord. To 'load' the crossbow, the end of the stock was placed on the ground, and the archer used all his weight to press the middle of the cord down towards the end of the stock, where it was fixed in a notch. The arrow or bolt fitted in a groove in the stock, and the crossbow was fired by pressing the string up from the notch in which it had been caught, to propel the missile along this groove.

In a later form of the crossbow, called the arbalest, an even greater tension of the string was secured by using a primitive sort of ratchet and a handle, with which to draw back the string to the farthest possible point. It was still necessary to put the stock on the ground, in order that the crossbowman might bear heavily on the ratchet as he wound up the string. This weapon, therefore, would not fire as fast as the ordinary bow.

The arbalest was one of the principal weapons of the Crusaders. Richard Coeur de Lion was particularly fond of it, and spent a large part of his income on mercenaries skilled in its use.

The ordinary bow, four or five feet long, became of so little importance that in 1181, when there was in England an Assize of Arms (a mustering of all the feudal levies to see that they possessed the equipment and weapons considered necessary), the bow was not mentioned as a weapon. But the following year, at Abergavenny, Welsh arrows penetrated an oak door four inches thick. And another Welsh arrow went through the skirt of a knight's mailed shirt, through his mailed breeches, his thigh, the wooden board that formed part of his saddle, and came to rest pinning knight and saddle firmly to his horse. These arrows were shot from long bows of elm, almost twice the size of ordinary bows. The English chronicler of this Welsh war described these bows as 'ugly unfinished-looking weapons, but astonishingly stiff, large and strong.'

For another hundred years the conservative English kings believed that the crossbow was a better weapon than the longbow. They employed Welsh archers occasionally, but probably these Welsh archers had no particular reason to wish to fight for English kings, and were not therefore very reliable troops. In 1281, we know from the pay-sheets of a castle held by the English in Wales, a crossbowman received four pence per day, a long-bowman received two pence.[1]

During their long, scrambling campaigns against fiery Welsh chiefs the English learned to use the longbow; but it scarcely developed into an important weapon until the first Plantagenet king, Edward the First, began the conquest of Scotland. The first invasion of this country was

[1] These were the official rates of pay, allowed to the chamberlain of the castle. But chamberlains did not always, in those days, act with complete altruism. If these soldiers got half their nominal wages, they were lucky.

an easy matter; the Scots had too few armoured knights to stand up to the English army, and very many of these knights chose to be on the English side.

A little later came a popular rebellion led by Wallace, an outlawed and obscure knight from the moors of Galloway. He won the whole of the Lowlands from the stupid sixty-year-old general whom Edward had left behind to keep control of Scotland. Next year, at Falkirk, Edward destroyed Wallace's army, which was almost entirely infantry and was deserted by its few noble horsemen, who even in those days did not like popular rebellions. To destroy the massed Scottish pikemen, Edward did not rely on his knights alone; when their first charge was checked, he brought forward his bowmen to pour their arrows into the Scottish ranks. The Scots could not reply; they had neither archers nor cavalry with which to hit back; their infantry dared not break ranks to go after the English archers; it was the last stage of Hastings over again. This weakness of infantry against the combination of heavy cavalry and archers was noted by a Scottish knight called Robert Bruce who was present at the battle on the English side.

The Scottish revolt went on. Bruce joined it, became its leader and King of Scotland. He fought a guerrilla war—the resource of national and popular movements in all ages. He advised his men to fight 'by hyll and mosse,' in the woods rather than in castles, by night surprises and ambushes; he 'scorched the earth,' burning crops to starve out the English armies, and gradually cleared the whole country until only three towns were in English hands.

Edward the First was dead, but in 1314 his half-baked son marched north to deal with the Bruce. The armies met at Bannockburn. Bruce had chosen a position guarded by woods and marshes so that only a very narrow front was open to the English attack. He was facing odds of two or three to one, and he had to rely on infantry against the heavy cavalry of the English. But the whole tactical lesson of the Welsh and Scottish wars—the value of the longbow when combined with troops capable of shock tactics—was ignored by the English army. Edward did not put archers in the gaps between formations of knights; the archers were set behind them. And the first line of the English knights, when their charge had failed and they could make no further progress uphill against the Scottish spears, were too stupid and too courageous to withdraw and try another charge. They did not even give room for their own second line of knights; they just piled up against the spears and went on hacking and hewing at them, while the second and third English lines waited on the slopes below without a chance of going into action.

Then the forgotten archers were remembered. But they could not be brought close to the Scots, because of all the uncontrollable mass of gentlemen packed into the narrow space in front of them. The archers were told to fire their arrows high in the air, and to try to reach the Scots over the heads of their own knights. The arrows hit far more English in the back than Scots in the breast. Eventually the English king fled, with a large bodyguard; left dead on the field of Bannockburn was a larger proportion of the English baronage than was slain in any battle before or after that time.

It was from this fighting in Scotland, and particularly from the massacre of Bannockburn, that the English army learned that a judicious use of the longbow was essential in battle and could make all the difference between victory and defeat. The application of this lesson at Crécy, thirty-two years later, began the destruction of feudalism, of the armoured knight, and of a whole period of war—the second armoured period.

The campaign that led to Crécy was a typical feudal raid, not so much aimed at decisive conquest as at the looting of French cities and at the lucrative business of capturing noble prisoners in battle, prisoners whose ransom built many fortunes in those days. This raid, led by Edward the Third, almost reached the walls of Paris. Edward then beat a hasty retreat in face of the much larger army that the French King brought against him. The crossing of the river Somme delayed Edward so long that the slow-moving feudal levies of the French were on his heels immediately after he had got across the river. Edward, although outnumbered by at least three to one, chose a strong defensive position on slightly rolling country where his archers could use their weapons to the best advantage.

Edward's army was, for a feudal army, very weak in armoured knights and very strong in archers. He probably had fewer than four thousand armoured men against the French twelve thousand or more; but he had over eleven thousand archers, and five thousand Welsh infantry, some of whom must have been archers, as against six thousand crossbowmen in French pay and a scrambling mass of roughly armed French infantry, among whom there can have been only a few bowmen.

The English archers were drawn up in a formation that they had learned in the Scottish and Welsh wars—a chessboard arrangement, often compared by the chroniclers to the way in which the teeth of a harrow are set. It was a relatively open formation, so that each man had room to see and fire between the gaps separating the men beside him or in front of him. Many of the archers seem to have been served by an aide, who carried equipment on the march and supplied them with a large reserve of arrows during battle. While waiting for the French, the archers and their aides dug in front of them small holes, a foot deep and a foot square, in which it was hoped that the horses of the French knights would stumble when they charged.

These archers were not strung out across the whole front of the position, but were concentrated on each wing, their lines sloping a little forward so that they faced inward; while between the two main 'battles' of men-at-arms that formed the English front line there was also a strong group of archers, behind whom were placed the infantry spearsmen. Farther back were the king's mounted reserves.

When the King of France received news that the English army was in sight, his own forces were spread out over ten or twelve miles of road from front to rear. He tried to check the advanced troops, but his feudal lords were quite without any idea of discipline: 'none of them would turn back, for each wished to be first in the field. The van halted, but those behind them kept riding forward, saying that they would get as far to the front as their fellows, and that from mere pride and jealousy. When the van saw the others pushing on, they would not be left behind, and without order or arrangement they pressed forward until they came in sight of the English.' That is Froissart's account of the beginning of the battle.

With the French King was the blind King of Bohemia and his son Charles, who called himself King of the Romans; there was the wild King of Majorca and a crowd of great gentlemen who had never taken orders in their lives. The only element of order and discipline in the French army were the six thousand Genoese crossbowmen. These mercenaries moved to the front, dressed their lines and began the action with a volley that fell short; firing uphill with fairly heavy projectiles, they had miscalculated the range.

The English replied with their longbows. Their weapon was more accurate as well as more powerful than the bows of previous centuries, and although it threw a slightly lighter shaft than the crossbow, it could be fired at least three times as fast and hit as hard or harder, having a higher muzzle velocity. It looked as if a snowstorm was beating on the Genoese, as the grey goose feathers caught the evening sun and the arrows pierced the leather surcoats and metal helmets of the crossbowmen.

The little ledge on which the English stood was only about a hundred and fifty feet above the shallow valley in front of them. But the ground curved in a way that was particularly convenient for projectile weapons. Looked at from the English position, most of the ground slopes at first very slightly; then the slope increases gradually; then it flattens out. A projectile, an arrow, falling more and more steeply as its speed fell oft, would follow the upper slope, keeping about the same height above the ground, to the flattening out. The archers were using 'grazing fire.'

From their ledge above the valley the English archers poured an unceasing rain of missiles upon the Genoese mercenaries, who were occupied with the complicated process of winding and ratcheting their crossbows. Disorder broke out among the Genoese, which so infuriated the mounted French knights waiting behind their bowmen's line that they attempted to retrieve this first check by an immediate charge, riding down a fair proportion of their own mercenaries. Some of these armoured horsemen managed to get through to the English right, but the effect of the arrow-fire told so heavily on their numbers that their charge achieved little but the unhorsing of the youthful Prince of Wales. All the front ranks of the French horsemen were broken, the animals fallen or stampeding about, riderless. Many an armoured knight was trampled, helpless, on the ground.

The French cavalry did not realise that the English archers had won the battle. Again and again they charged as if sheer weight of horses and men could win home in spite of the confusion and the continuous deadly fire of the longbows. As each charge came, it met the missile defence and was broken, adding to the welter of dead and maddened mounts, of fallen men and knights. One charge reached one end of the English line, where it encountered and failed to pass a barricade of wagons. Finally, the King of France himself led a great body to the centre, but neither he nor any of his lieges could force his horse against the unremitting fire of the English infantry. Well into the hours of darkness the archers stood in unbroken line, steadily supplied with ammunition and easily making up their few losses.

The remaining French knights rode away. The English line moved forward to loot and to look over the faces of the dead. On Saturday night, August 26, 1346, the battle of Crécy ended. One thousand five hundred French knights had fallen.

The victory of Crécy, and a later victory at Poictiers, made the fighting reputation of the English on the Continent. In previous times Continental military leaders had looked down upon the English as poor soldiers. 'In my youth,' wrote the Italian, Petrarch, 'the Britons that they call Angles or English passed for the most timid of barbarian nations; now they are a most warlike nation. She [England] has overturned the ancient military glory of France by victories so numerous and so unexpected that they who lately were inferior to the miserable Scots, besides the lamentable and undeserved catastrophe that I cannot think of without sighing, have so upset things by their mettle and by that of the whole kingdom, that I, who last crossed it on my business, had difficulty in persuading myself that it was the same country that I had formerly seen.'[2]

[2] Quoted by Field, *Old Time Under Arms* (1939), page 5.

It looks to me as if the second armoured period began because the Franks of Charlemagne's day were far from what was then the centre of civilisation (Byzantium and the lands round it, and the empire of Mahomet's followers). Isolated to some extent in their end of Europe, these Franks became the first modern nation-state, uniting the qualities taught by long Roman occupation to those of the 'barbarians' who had broken Rome. And perhaps in the same way the second armoured period ended because the English, even more isolated beyond the narrow seas, learned in Wales and Scotland to make of the bow a far better weapon than it had ever been before.

The best-trained horse-archers of Byzantium had learned that the bow cord must be drawn to the ear, not to the breast or shoulder. When the cord is drawn to the ear, the eye can look along the arrow. Saracen archers learned this also; but horse-archers' bows are short, and when armour became strong enough to resist most arrows, archery fell into disesteem, and this way of aiming was forgotten. A horseman could not carry a longbow; nor could he easily use his whole strength, pulling a bow, when mounted.

The Welsh and English rediscovered the secret of accurate aim; and they used the heaviest longbow known, practising with it until they could drive their arrows accurately at the less well-armoured parts of their targets. Their arrows could often pierce normal armour, not only because of the high 'muzzle velocity' of the missiles, but because armour had become too 'refined.' It had gradually become more and more complete, covering the whole of a man and much of his horse; but this completeness was gained at the expense of a lightening of the material. A horse can only carry so much weight; if the armour is spread out, to cover all the man and much of the horse, it has to be made thinner. Chain-mail was becoming delicate. In much of the knight's armour it was replaced by metal plates, that might be stronger in themselves than chain-mail, but could have dangerous gaps between them.

The English archers scored particularly heavily against the horses of the opposing forces, despite the fact that horses were now more often protected than they had been. Though we have little good information, it seems very probable that the heavy cavalry these archers defeated were so loaded with armour that they could not go faster than a slow trot. They could no longer charge at the gallop, as heavy cavalry had done at previous times. While this is uncertain, it is quite clear that armour had become so heavy that any knight unhorsed was likely to be useless for further fighting.

A knight floundering on his back might be unable to get up, because of the stiffness and weight of his kit. A knight unhorsed would hit the ground so massively that he was 'out' from shock for some time. The pitiful inadequacy of the knight off his horse, very like the inadequacy of some sea-beast stranded, was shown at the next important encounter after Crécy, that of Poictiers (1356).

In this battle almost all the French knights rode to the field of action, but then dismounted and tried to fight on foot. Because they moved so ponderously slowly on foot, each division or 'battle' of their army came into action alone, after the one before it had been beaten. And many of these knights seem to have been physically exhausted by their march before they struck a blow.

At the smaller battle of Auray (1364) both sides dismounted. The side that won had kept a small reserve of two hundred mounted men-at-arms, who seem to have ridden their horses when moving tactically, then to have dismounted to fight. Oman writes of this action that the commander of this reserve force, Calverley, made his men 'strip off their cuissarts [thigh-pieces] to allow them to move about more easily—a proof that the full knightly armour had now grown heavy enough to make all motion difficult when the wearer had been wearied by long fighting. Without this expedient his reserve would not have been moveable enough for use at each point of the line, as it was successively in danger of being broken through.'[3]

With these combats the man on horseback no longer ruled warfare. And while he was being defeated by the longbow in France, he was falling to other weapons in Switzerland, where the burghers, in their fight to free themselves from the German feudal lords, had formed their leagues and cantons. During the fourteenth and fifteenth centuries they fought frequent battles against the German Empire and the Burgundians. The Swiss fighters were plain townsmen and cowherds, 'ill-conditioned, rough and bad peasant folk, in whom there is found no virtue, no noble blood, and no moderation,' as the Emperor Maximilian somewhat petulantly asserted. But despite these social shortcomings they proved themselves to be some of the toughest fighters in Europe.

Finding that their spears were of little use against the heavier lances of the knights, the Swiss contrived a new weapon, the halberd. This was a combination of axe and spear, having a sharp point for thrusting at a knight, a heavy axe for smashing down on his helmeted head, and a curved hook for yanking him off his charger. This halberd was the first special weapon of democracy. It gave the Swiss cantons their independence and the Swiss people their custom—still in force—by which each citizen keeps his own weapon in his own home. The halberd became the weapon carried by royal guards throughout Western Europe, because it was a weapon that helped to destroy the power of the feudal barons and therefore made royal power real.

[3] Oman, *op. cit.*, page 636.

Though the leaders of the English and Swiss at this period were nobles, the relationship of the men to their leaders was not entirely that of feudal allegiance. More often it was a far more modern relationship: that of cash. More and more, the feudal levies were being superseded by archers who were hired professional soldiers, who fought for a wage and looked drily upon the outdated and high-falutin' notions of glory still exploited by their overlords.

Then came gunpowder to complete the process of remaking the ways of war, and gradually to end the use of armour. The use of powder was discovered, in Europe, in the thirteenth century, some say by Roger Bacon. The first 'musket' or 'hand-gun' appeared in the fifteenth century. Gunpowder used in larger weapons blasted the foundations of that stronghold of feudalism, the castle. Not only could the knight be put out of battle by a musket or cannon ball, before he could strike a blow, but the feudal lord and his people were no longer secure behind their fortifications. Gunpowder was a leveller. It made the townsman, the merchant, the craftsman or apprentice, and the peasant and professional soldier equal in combat with the seigneur. The days of chivalry were passing fast, and many were those among the knighthood who felt the yearning of Don Quixote:

> Blessed be those happy ages that were strangers to the dreadful fury of these devilish instruments of artillery, whose inventor I am satisfied is now in Hell, receiving the reward of his cursed invention, which is the cause that very often a cowardly base hand takes away the life of the bravest gentleman, and that in the midst of that vigour and resolution which animates and inflames the bold, a

> chance bullet (shot perhaps by one that fled, and was frightened at the very flash the mischievous piece gave when it went off), coming nobody knows how or from whence, in a moment puts a period to the brave designs and the life of one that deserved to have survived many years. This considered, I could almost say, I am sorry at heart for having taken upon me this profession of a knight-errant, in so detestable an age; for though no danger daunts me, yet it affects me to think, whether powder and lead may not deprive me of the opportunity of becoming famous, and making myself known throughout the world by the strength of my arm, and dint of my sword.[4]

The hostility of the ruling caste to guns and gunnery lasted long. As, step by step, gunpowder changed the whole aspect of warfare, the die-hards and brass-hats of those days fought their losing battle with a tenacity worthy of better ends. Like most people who detest in innovation, they believed, or affected to believe, that the innovators were immoral or infidel. Even in 1676, an English writer began his dissertation, 'A Light on the Art of Gunnery,' as follows: 'The reason, wherefore my first discourse is of Gunners, is only because many times it falleth out, that most men employed for Gunners, are very negligent of the fear of God.'

I should hate to hazard a guess as to the truth of this statement. But it was clearly true, for generations after generations of fighting men, that gunners were thought of as specially terrible fellows, likely to be in league with

[4] Cervantes, *Don Quixote,* Everyman's Edition, Volume 1, pp. 318-19.

the Devil. And it was also true that the armoured fighting men tried every way they could to suppress or circumvent them. And men clung to their armour for centuries after it had lost fighting value. In 1807, the Tsar of all the Russias used against Napoleon's armies, in Poland, fifteen hundred Bashkirs wearing chain-mail and armed with bows and arrows. They were as valueless for fighting as the Lancers of the Viceroy of India are today.

Among the toy soldiers I played with as a child there were some specially proud and haughty horsemen called Life Guards. They, and their natural enemies, the French Cuirassiers, wore breastplates of steel. It was the thrill of my young life to see these toy soldiers, come alive, very big, and clattering most impressively, ride down from Buckingham Palace before the first Great War. But they were toy soldiers: when I saw them, in 1912, the great period of the armoured man on horseback was five hundred years away; the last armoured knights of Europe had charged the Turk three hundred years before.

5
Castle and Gunpowder

One of the things I have deliberately left out of this book until this chapter has been fortification. Throughout the history of warfare sieges have often been among the most important types of battles, and have often been decisive. Now that we have reached, in our history, the beginnings of gunpowder, it will be as well to go back through the past periods and note some parallels in the development of siegecraft to the tendencies already described.

The walled and defended city has existed since there were cities; in fact, the first growth of cities was probably as much for defence as for other social ends. During the first unarmoured period it seems probable that the walled city or little town was the only normal fortification. There were a few less permanent fortifications; the Greeks besieging Troy built barriers of some sort to protect their ships and the camp alongside it. But these 'field fortifications' were rare and would normally only occur in the case of sieges.

Assault on fortifications was always difficult in this period, and was usually undertaken by trick—the Trojan Horse—or by a straight storming of the walls or gates. Battering-rams must have been used early in history, usually against gates; but we have no knowledge of other 'machines' until we get to the first armoured period.

Armour permitted the attacking force to get near to the defenders; the defenders were, of course, sheltered by the walls, and armour gave to the attackers a similar though weaker protection. The first development during the period of the armoured foot-soldier that we need to note is the use of tight-packed shields covering a group of men who approached the wall or gate under this cover. Soon this became the *testudo* or tortoise, a regular military formation for the job. The shields linked together looked like the scales of a tortoise. Much later the same purpose would be served by a penthouse or moveable hut, usually made of hides, later still of tiles and hurdles covered with earth; this was used as a protective roof to protect attacking forces from the arrows and burning liquids and heavy stones showered down upon them from the walls.

Protected by their shields or by such a covering, the attacking forces would bring forward their ram, which at first would be carried and swung simply by men's hands. It might easily be the largest tree of the countryside near the city. Later it was found more efficient to support the weight of the ram on two perpendicular beams and on ropes or chains from these beams; then fewer men could swing the ram farther and with more effect.

Besides the rams there were other 'engines,' some of which we shall describe later. These engines were hard to move, and usually easier to construct in their emplacement for the defence of a city than to build elsewhere for the attack on the city. We have already mentioned the development of these machines about 300 b.c., and the use of some of them by Alexander the Great as a field artillery. As the armoured period developed away from the simple solidity of a homogeneous army, and towards more complexity and coordination, there was a considerable increase in the numbers and importance of these machines. In 149 b.c., when Carthage surrendered, the Romans claimed the capture of two thousand catapults from the Carthaginian Army and from its stores in the city. This means that there was probably one stone-throwing 'piece of artillery' for every hundred soldiers in the Carthaginian Army. This is quite a high proportion of artillery to troops; just to take a comparison, Wellington's army at Waterloo had one gun for rather more than four hundred men.

Carthage probably had this considerable amount of artillery because it was a trading and commercial and mechanical empire; machinery is a natural product of craftsmanship and large-scale production for trade. Syracuse, before Carthage, was also a great commercial city; and it was in Syracuse that artillery seems first to have become important. At the time when Rome destroyed Carthage, the Romans seem to have had relatively little artillery, but when Rome replaced her rival as the centre of the world's trade and the monopolist of its most ingenious products, the Romans began to give their soldiers more and more 'machines.' About two centuries after the fall of Carthage, the full equipment of a legion of six thousand men consisted of ten catapults and sixty *carroballistae*. The latter were light field pieces mounted on wheels, and the legion would take them with it wherever wheels could move. The catapults, on the other hand, were heavier machines, normally used only for the defence of fortifications and for the attack upon them.

The first portable fortification of importance in warfare were the stakes carried by the Roman legions. Each legionary on the march carried a long hardened stake of wood, and when the legions went into camp they planted these stakes to make a fence or wall, and also if possible dug a deep ditch outside the wall.

The Roman entrenched camp was a definite part of the Roman tactics. Its wall provided a safe base in which the whole of a Roman force could rest, and from which it could send out detachments or line up for battle as a whole. The surrounding ditches were often fifteen to twenty feet wide; sometimes a second outer ditch would be cut and a road left between the two along which the Romans could move their troops if they desired. Eventually a linked system of fortifications of this sort, protecting the Roman Empire from German invasion, stretched for three hundred and seventy-five miles from Neuwied on the Rhine to Ratisbon on the Danube. This *limes Germanicus* was the Maginot Line of its day. It lasted longer than the Maginot Line. It did not last forever.

When Julius Caesar made a camp on Mont Saint-Pierre, in the Forest of Compiègne,

> he caused an earthwork to be thrown up twelve feet high with a parapet and ordered that two ditches, fifteen feet deep, be dug in front of it. He built a great number of three-storeyed towers, linked together with bridges and circular platforms protected by wicker screens, so that the enemy advance was held up by a double fosse and two lines of defenders. The first line was ranged on the upper platforms, whence, better sheltered and overtopping the others, the soldiers hurled their darts greater distances with greater safety. The second line, ranged behind the parapet and closer to the enemy, was protected from their barbs by those who fought on the platform above.

In another case, when Caesar drew trench lines to block an army of Gauls into the town of Alesia, he dug special trenches five feet deep and planted the bottom of these trenches with sharp wooden spikes. In front of these he had smaller traps made, about three feet deep, in which the stakes were so hidden that they protruded for only a foot. Briars and other bushes were grown to hide these stakes; the whole effect must have been very like that of a well-kept barbed-wire entanglement in modern warfare. His men seem to have shifted about two million cubic metres of earth to make the trenches.

The Roman legion, when properly entrenched, was scarcely ever successfully attacked by its opponents. It had, therefore, the immense advantage of being able to wait safely within its camp until some diversion had divided the opposing forces or until some addition of strength had reached the Roman commander.

The Romans not only used their stakes for the camps that were their main military fortifications. They used them also for minor tactical jobs, such as the blocking or narrowing of a ford. If you are foolish enough to go swimming tomorrow in a shallow and muddy patch of the Thames, not far from Brentford, at very low water, you may hit your foot on a fire-hardened stake of wood; there are still a few of these stakes in the river bed, put there by Roman soldiers nearly two thousand years ago. This part of the river was once fordable, as the name Brentford tells us. The Roman sentinels sent to guard this ford, as the legions were pushing up through Britain, narrowed it with their stakes so that the enemy could cross at one point only. And when the Roman Empire settled down to fairly permanent frontiers along the *limes Germanicus,* the general idea of Roman fortification degenerated from the camp, organised for all-round defence, to the line of stakes or entrenchments spread as a thin linear crust over hundreds of miles of territory.

If you had gone to the Maginot Line in 1939, you would have seen stakes very like these Roman stakes, made out of new materials, but arranged fundamentally in the same way, Part of this line was defended by 'iron asparagus,' long lines of steel rails, cemented into the earth so that their ends stood up like jagged spikes. These were barriers against tanks. They were not arranged as the Roman camp had been, for all-round defence of areas from which a striking force could be launched; they were arranged as the later fortifications of the decaying Empire were laid out—mainly as a thin line, and once that line was pierced, its value went.

The Romans built walls across England and southern Scotland, as the Chinese two or three hundred years before them had built a Great Wall to keep out the raiding tribes of the North. But these walls were not at first intended to be garrisoned in such a way that the enemy was always kept beyond them. They were permanent obstacles to any raider; but their main military value was that they prevented a raiding party getting back home with the loot. Burdened with animals and stores, the raiders would try to return, and would be caught by detachments from the garrisons on each side of the point where they had broken through. When the raiders became strong enough to become invaders, when Goths or Germans wanted not only to break into the Empire, but to stay in it, these walls lost much of their value and significance. But because those who created them came to rely on them more and more, at these same periods a larger proportion of the active defending troops were tied to these wall lines with all the disadvantages of passive defence.

When the Roman legion became a wall garrison of relative unimportance, it was destroyed; and with it ended the Roman camp. Also, by one of the ironies of history, the classical artillery that had developed so much came to an end at the same time. This artillery had been one of the factors that, to use a philosophical term, 'negated' the Roman legion; it was itself negated by the ending of the

Roman legion. It was too clumsy to accompany an army of horse-archers. It was too heavy to be moved by roads when the good Roman roads fell into disrepair. It found no useful targets: cavalry in open order were poor targets and fleeting ones; and there were no longer many important fortifications at which it could hammer. The only fortifications left were the cities, and these became—with the breakdown of the Roman peace—small, poor, scarcely worth robbing.

Then, 'out of the spent and unconsidered earth the cities rise again.' And first the ram comes back into warfare, and then other engines are invented or remembered for the assault on cities and later on the medieval castles.

The ram was always a clumsy instrument and could normally only batter a hole in a single line of fortifications. If there was a double line, one wall behind the other, the men handling the ram would get into great difficulties as soon as they had breached the first wall. When a city or castle was well defended, the outer wall would be lower than the inner wall, and the attackers who seized a portion of it would find themselves still exposed to a fire against which they had no reply. The men trying to use the battering-ram against the defenders of the second wall would generally be subjected to a fire from three sides. Their usual recourse, against such systems of walls, was to build a ramp that brought them to the same level as the defenders, or to build towers that they could move up to the walls, in order to fire down on the defenders from the tops of these towers. These had to be made of wood and could be set on fire.

When rams were employed in the siege of Jerusalem in 1099, the defenders used forked beams to push the ram to one side or downward so that it could not be swung. They also used great pads of sacking which they lowered with ropes from the tops of the walls to act as buffers; the rams hit against these pads, instead of against the parts of the wall that previous blows had weakened.

The development of the ram and of the bore (a long pole with a sharp iron point rotated to pierce a wall) made it necessary for fortifications to consist of two or more strong concentric perimeters. Usually the cities in the Dark Ages and in the early Middle Ages were too poor to keep up, or even to attempt to build, this solid double fortification around them. Therefore, for most military purposes the keep or castle, within the city or not far from it, became of greater importance than the walls of the city itself. Sometimes the castle, as at Lincoln, would be big enough for most of the citizens to take shelter within it if a raiding enemy appeared who might pierce the city walls. And as feudalism developed, the feudal nobility built their own castles, either where they themselves lived or at strategic points in their territory. These fortifications, organised for all-round defence, can be considered the natural military forms of fortification in the period when a small striking force of armoured knights was the main factor in battle. And like the Roman camps they were, from a military point of view, secure bases from which a striking force could emerge at the right moment for battle.

Here, then, is a striking parallel between the two armoured periods that we have been considering: in each case the high point in military fortification is a camp or castle organised for all-round defence and intended to hold out for some period when surrounded by the enemy. It is not a line, but an 'island of resistance.' We shall see this principle of fortification return when we come to the third armoured period, that of the tank.

Two weapons already mentioned, the ram and the bore, were mainly responsible for the doubling of medieval walls. Other weapons forced further development.

The siege-tower, with crossbowmen or small catapults upon it that could bring fire to bear against defenders on top of high walls, made it necessary for the second wall to be spaced farther away from the first. Ludwig Renn makes this very clear in his book on the relation of war to society:

> As the range of arms throwing a projectile improved, the distance between the two walls had to be increased. The defensive walls of Constantinople lie very close together, indeed, whereas the distance between the defensive walls of Marienburg in East Prussia, one of the fortresses of a knightly order, is considerably greater, because this fortress was built towards the close of the Middle Ages, when the crossbow, which shot considerably farther than the ordinary bow, was already in use. The distance between the defensive walls of Nuremberg is greater still, because the fortress there was built at a time when firearms were already in use.

And Renn concludes:

> Here we have a principle of fortification which still retains its validity today for defences built in a series of lines: the distance from line to line is determined by the fire range of the attacker.[1]

[1] Ludwig Renn, *Warfare, the Relation of War to Society,* page 119.

Besides the crossbow, and probably before it, the men of the Dark Ages and of the Middle Ages had a much bigger and clumsier machine made in the same shape. The cord was pulled back by small hand winches, and this machine threw bolts or javelins with a fairly flat trajectory. Another type of machine, more like a howitzer than a gun, was the mangon. It was developed from the machine that the ancient Romans called the *onager,* or wild ass, probably because it leapt off the ground with all four feet when released. This consisted of a wooden base from which rise two stout posts between which were twisted a double or quadruple set of ropes. A beam was then twisted into the ropes in such a way that when one end of it was hauled back, the torsion of the ropes exerted a very considerable force to rotate the beam. A spoon-shaped hole was made at one end of the beam, or a sling attached to it, in which the engineer placed the projectile—a rock or a ball of lead. When the machine was 'fired' by releasing the beam, the ropes, untwisting, would throw the projectile high in the air over the walls that were being attacked.

During the twelfth and thirteenth centuries a slightly more accurate machine, called the *trébuchet,* became the main siege engine. It consisted of a long horizontal pole, balanced on a pivot supported by two uprights placed much nearer the butt end of the pole than the working end. These uprights raised the pole some way from the ground. The working end, the longer part of the pole, was pulled down to the ground and held down by catches, then the missile was placed in the spoon-shaped hole in it or in a sling. The butt end was loaded with heavy weights of iron and stone, fixed in a kind of box, or in some cases bound to the pole with cords. When the catches were released, these weights pulled the butt end down, and the other end of the seesaw flung the projectile high and fairly far.

Trenches were seldom used by besieging parties in these days, but breastworks of twisted hurdle, generally covered with a coating of hide, were used to make covered ways of approach to the 'batteries' or to the enemy walls. And mining and countermining played an increasing part in siegecraft; the besieging forces would try to mine under a piece of wall, propping up their workings with timber; then they would set the timber afire and hope that part of the walls would collapse. This method of attack was used by Philip of Macedon when he besieged Constantinople in 340 b.c.; exactly the same method was sometimes used by Crusaders fifteen hundred years later. But mining did not become really important until gunpowder was understood and could be used for it. In 1503, at Naples, Peter of Navarre successfully blew up part of a castle by means of powder. Mining remained a hazardous business. The attackers had to dig deep under moat and castle, and the defenders might flood the hole from the moat or dig through on their own side to fight hand-to-hand in the dark.

The weakest point in any fortification is normally the ordinary point of entry, the gate. The ram was used against a gate when possible; wooden gates of medieval castles could be set on fire or a mine driven under the gate towers. When gunpowder came into use, a special form of portable mine for blowing in gates was invented; it was called the *petard*. It was a heavy metal bowl or pot in the shape of a big top hat, which was filled with powder and either spiked onto the wooden gate of a castle or propped against it with stone or wooden backing. When the fuse had been lighted, the force of the explosion blew the gates inward—and the petard outward towards the attackers. The unwary engineer who stayed too long or too close, after the fuse had been lighted, could be 'hoist with his own petard.'

In those Elizabethan days, 'when the world was so new and all,' even the high command new and not averse to new weapons, a British force went into action, according to a contemporary ballad:

> 'With a new shippe and a new Generall
> And a new noble Lord High Admirall
> With a new device to batter an oulde walle
> And a new peatarre to make the gate falle[2]

Before we deal further with gunpowder, Greek fire should be mentioned. This has been described as 'wet fire' and is said to have been invented by a Greek named Callinicus in the seventh century. It was mainly composed of sulphur and quicklime, which took fire when exposed to moisture and was projected through a siphon or nozzle. Sometimes arrows were dipped in it before firing, or huge pots containing it were flung on board enemy vessels. The fires caused were extremely difficult to put out. At the siege of Acre in 1190 by the Crusaders, a Damascene engineer burned all the siege-machines of the invaders by flinging jars of the fluid upon them. Earlier, in the year 717, the great Arab leader Maslama, brother of the Caliph Suleiman, was attacking Constantinople in the campaigns to extend the Empire of Islam. He attempted a land attack, but it proved hopeless in face of the fortifications of the Byzantine engineers. So Maslama entrenched his army, surrounding his camp with a deep ditch, and resolved to compel the surrender of Leo the Isaurian, Emperor of Byzantium, by blockading Constantinople. He instructed his brother Suleiman to send a squadron of ships to force their way through the Bosphorus and proceed northward to cut the city off from supplies from the towns on the Black Sea. This squadron arrived in September, 717,

[2] Field, *op. cit.*, page 16.

and got under way to sail north of the Golden Horn. There lay Leo's fleet in harbour, protected by the great chain suspended between two towers from each side of the harbour's entrance. As the blockading ships came round Seraglio Point, they were thrown out of line by the strong current. Immediately Leo ordered the chain to be lowered and his galleys sailed out and poured Greek fire on the enemy's ships, destroying twenty and capturing others. The attack was so well directed and so decisive that it largely contributed to the defeat of the blockade.

Greek fire was an excellent defensive weapon against besiegers, used in reply to the catapulted stones and balls of lead projected over the castle walls by the early siege-engines, such as the *ballista* and the *trébuchet*. These remained the great weapons of siege artillery until the invention of gunpowder. Then came the period of the bombard or mortar and the gun or cannon.

Bombards were used as siege weapons, to throw projectiles in a high trajectory over walls, and cannon as flat-trajectory weapons for direct discharge against walls. Cannon needed large amounts of gunpowder; they also had to have long barrels, so they developed rather slowly. Towards the end of the Middle Ages, cannon were used in the field. At the battle of Crécy the English army used two guns; it is in the records that the army had only twelve gunners. Warring against the Swiss, the Duke of Burgundy used cannon mounted on wagons, but they were not very successful. In the middle of the fifteenth century, Eastern armies began to demonstrate the qualities of the new 'pots' or bombards in siege warfare.

In 1453, the Turks under the Sultan Mohammed II—the Conqueror—besieged Constantinople. Mohammed's artillery was formidable, his best bombards being cast for him by a Hungarian cannon-founder named Urban. These guns threw stone shot thirty inches in diameter and weighing twelve hundred to eighteen hundred pounds. Each 'howitzer' required sixty oxen to drag it, two hundred men to march alongside to keep it in position, and two hundred more men to level the road. Mohammed had a total of fourteen batteries, consisting of thirteen great bombards and fifty-six smaller weapons of all kinds. This artillery greatly assisted in the Turkish conquest of Constantinople. And these guns lasted a long time. One of the Turkish guns of 1453 survived till 1807, when the seven-hundred-pound ball it projected shattered a mast of Admiral Duckworth's flagship in the Napoleonic Wars.

Even heavier projectiles were known. The Venetians in the fourteenth century produced a shell consisting of two hemispheres of stone or bronze, filled with gunpowder, and fired by primitive fuses attached to it, which hissed as they went through the air. These shells sometimes weighed as much as three thousand pounds, according to reports accepted by the historians.

Incendiary shells were also used in the fifteenth century, to set fire to wooden buildings. Sometimes flares were fired in order to light up the enemy lines for the pikemen. Fireballs were also used to blind the enemy. These were solid balls of metal heated in a furnace before being projected. Some of these 'shells' were designed to break up in small pieces when they struck an object. There were, in addition, forms of case-shot, large numbers of small pellets fired straight at the infantry.

While the cannon fulfilled the purpose of the ancient ram, the mortar or bombard was the gunpowder version of the *trébuchet*. The mortar usually had a very short and thick barrel and looked like a pot. The chief advantage of the mortar lay in its relative lightness. And it was nearly always easier to fire effectively over the top of walls, causing damage within, than to destroy them by continual pounding at the outside.

We have already seen how feudalism, the regime based on the power of an armoured cavalry, suffered its first defeats at the hands of the yeomen archers. These men, working for pay, professional soldiers rather than feudal retainers, were the forerunners of new social forces and new classes that were preparing to destroy and remake the feudal world. The ending of feudalism and of armour did not occur rapidly. Cromwell's soldiers were 'Ironsides' and wore a heavy breastplate designed to turn a pistol bullet. At the same period John Sobieski, who became King of Poland by his victories over the Turks, was fighting with a heavily armoured cavalry, some of whom wore heavy metal 'wings' designed to make a loud noise as they rode; the noise was intended to frighten the enemy. Some of these Polish knights were strapped to their saddles so that they could not fall off even if wounded: this heavy cavalry was used as a shock force that could break through any infantry line opposed to it.

But long before this, in places less out of the way than Britain or Poland, firearms were beginning to master armour and at the same time to master the castle. The social results of this were first emphasised by Friedrich Engels in his *Anti-Duhring* (page 190):

> Firearms required industry and money, and both of these were in the hands of the burghers of the towns. From the outset, therefore, firearms were the weapons of the towns, and of the rising monarchy drawing its support from the towns, against the feudal nobility. The stone walls of the nobleman's castles, hitherto unapproachable, fell before the cannon of the burghers, and the bullets of the burghers' arquebuses pierced the armour of the knights. With the armour-clad cavalry of

> the feudal lords, the feudal lords' supremacy was also broken; with the development of the bourgeoisie, infantry and guns became more and more the decisive types of weapons.

In the next chapter we deal with the development of the musket and of field artillery. In this chapter on siegecraft we need to note that the use of gunpowder gradually decreased the importance of the castle, but at the same time the growing wealth of towns increased for a period the importance of the strongly fortified town. Cities as big as London or Paris could no longer be strongly defended; they were too large, and they were always spreading beyond their walls. But little stable fortress towns, such as Toumay or Badaioz, became of increasing importance and were for a time almost the only form of fortification that mattered much in warfare. The defences of these towns at first developed in the direction of complicated outworks. The fire of the defenders' cannon could not be directed so easily to the foot of the walls from little balconies built out from those walls, as the fire of more primitive weapons had been. It was therefore necessary to push out salients in front of the walls, strong-points that were called 'horn-works' or 'redans.' From these the defenders' artillery could fire to the flank along the walls and prevent the attackers' approach to them. But gradually it became impossible to expect ordinary stonework to stand up to the destructive effect of improving artillery. Napoleon Bonaparte, writing a précis of the wars of Julius Caesar, pointed out that 'the arms of the ancient world . . . called for upstanding strong points with high towers and walls; modern arms make necessary low forts covered with slopes of earth that mask the masonry.'

With this development we reach the beginning of modern fortifications, to be dealt with later in this book.

6
Musket and Bayonet

Few of the weapons that we have been describing have any modern interest to us. Modern mortars and guns have developed directly from the first bombards and cannon; but sword and spear and battle-axe have gone into the discard of time, the arrow has gone, and with these weapons have passed away the tactics and formations of the armies using them. Here at the entry to modern war, war of firearms, infantry, field artillery, it is worth while repeating that some of the patterns of modern war are parallel to those of the past: in new and more complicated forms the same processes work through to similar conclusions. In the modern unarmoured period that we have now to consider, the first main process was the slow development of an army that could hit like a single heavy hammer.

We have seen this process before during armoured periods. Fighting mainly by shock weapons, the armoured infantry of classical times or the armoured knights of the Middle Ages first grouped their forces into phalanxes, with which they could break through an opposing line. Why does this process come back again in an unarmoured period? In the previous unarmoured period, after the defeat of the legion, there had been no such development.

The answer seems to be that the new weapons were too heavy and clumsy to be carried on horseback, and only a few could be pulled on wheels. Therefore, the change away from the shock tactics typical of an armoured period was gradual; it did not come fully for three or four hundred years. During those years 'unarmoured shock' developed. Therefore, the defeat of the armoured knight and the steadily increasing importance of infantry implied a reduction in tactical mobility. In the previous unarmoured period the horse-archer had been tactically mobile; the musketeer was much less mobile. And there was another change that made shock weapons of considerable importance during the time that armour was gradually being wiped out; the musket, which was very slow to fire, was substituted for the bow and arrow which fired rapidly. (The longbow in skilful hands could keep several arrows in the air, one following the other.)

Opposition to the change from bow to musket was powerful. As an example, Colonel Sir John Smyth wrote to the Privy Council in 1591: 'The bow is a simple weapon, firearms are very complicated things which get out of order in many ways . . . a very heavy weapon and tires out soldiers on the march. Whereas also a bowman can let off six aimed shots a minute, a musketeer can discharge but one in two minutes.' Many other John Smiths felt the same distrust of the new arms.

Men equipped with the first primitive firearms had only a chance to fire once against an enemy charging them. Defence by longbow could almost be defence by fire alone; when firearms were the principal weapons of the defence, they had to be strongly supported by shock weapons for use at close quarters. Otherwise the line of musketeers was likely to be caught while loading and unable to fire.

The principal shock weapon of the period was the pike—a spear used, not so much for thrusting as the ancient spears had been, but more as a portable fortification. The infantry of a medieval army had also contained a number of men with pikes, but when the bow was given up and the new clumsy expensive firearms came in, the proportion between men armed with projectile weapons and men armed with these shock weapons altered. The firearms were at first few; the pikes were many. For these reasons the opening part of the unarmoured period of modern war shows some of the characteristics of an armoured period: importance of shock weapons and the development of drilled, homogenous heavy forces, to which light forces were auxiliaries. This is in briefest summary the period from the first firearms up to the army of Frederick the Great.

The first firearms were, as I have stated, greatly disliked by the foremost soldiers of the day. An entirely unambiguous attitude towards them was taken by the Chevalier Bayard, whose name is still a symbol for noble soldiering; of Bayard the phrase was first coined, 'without fear and without reproach.' He considered it correct and Christian to hack at a man with a sword or run him through with a spear; these were things that had always been done. But it was devilish to shoot him from a distance; it was unfair that the anonymous churl, with an iron tube and some gunpowder and a great slug of lead, could abolish a knight before the knight realised what was happening. Therefore, the Chevalier when he took prisoner any man who, by his dress or equipment, could be seen to have carried a firearm, hanged his prisoner on the spot.

The first firearm was a short metal tube with a straight stick roughly fixed to it. The stick was held under the arm when firing, and the weapon was, as we should say now, 'fired from the hip.' Actually it was fired with the stick between the armpit and the hip. This hand-gun, later arquebus, had a small hole in the side of the barrel into which a pinch of gunpowder was shaken after the weapon had been loaded from the muzzle end. Loading was a job;

the soldier had to hold his weapon vertically and pour into it a measured quantity of rough-grained powder. Then he took a thick wad and rammed it down on top of the powder. Then he dropped down the slug or ball, which was usually so roughly shaped that it would jam and have to be forced down with a ramrod. It was often necessary to put another wad on top of this, if the projectile was at all loose in the barrel; if this second wad was not put in, the projectile might, when the weapon was being moved or levelled, slide down the barrel or even fall out of it.

Powder was usually carried in a horn, and the weight of charge had to be guessed. There were no neat little cartridges each containing the correct weight of propellant. There was therefore, very little uniformity about the range of the weapon; and powder might be damp and not give much more than a fizzle. The muzzle velocity was low, even if the powder was dry and correctly shaped and sized; and so the shot had to be a large one. A light bullet travelling slowly would not have gone through armour. For this reason the calibre of the old arquebus and of the musket that followed it was far greater than that of the modern rifle; it was more like that of a twelve-bore shotgun.

The arquebus could usually propel its heavy projectile between two hundred and three hundred yards. But this was extreme range, and normally it would be used at less than sixty yards. At twenty yards a skilled man could hit a small haystack, or a group of four men riding abreast. Then it was discovered that if the barrel was made longer, the charge of powder increased, and the projectile moulded more carefully, fire could be a little more accurate at longer ranges. And the Spaniards introduced the first real musket, about the middle of the sixteenth century. It fired a lead ball weighing about one and a half ounces.

The barrel of the musket was of much heavier gauge than that of the arquebus—and also longer, in order to use the full force of the propellant, which burned fairly slowly—so that the weapon was at first too heavy for a man to fire it without some support. Each musketeer had an assistant who carried his weapon before action, and during action helped him to prop it on a specially made pole, one end of which was stuck in the ground. Experiments were also made with a two-legged pole, like the bipod mounting of a modern light machine-gun. It was found inefficient to balance the weapon on a pole which was connected to it at its centre of gravity; this allowed the weapon to slew about too much. These props were therefore normally at the far end of the barrel, and the musketeer took half the weight of his 'engine.' It soon became clear that it was easier for him to have the powder-pan, which he had to light, high up rather than low down; therefore, he must put his weapon to his shoulder rather than tuck one end of it under his arm. So early muskets had the first roughly shaped stocks. The weapon, however, was still so inaccurate that there was not much point in looking along it, for aiming, and therefore the stock was not so shaped as to bring the barrel up to the level of a man's eye.

It will be remembered that the full development of the bow and arrow came only with the longbow, which was so tall that the man wielding it had to pull the string back to his eye or ear and therefore could look along the arrow for aim. In the same way the full development of the musket came only when the weapon had been used for a long time, had been accepted by the nobility and gentry, and was made in particularly fine and hand-wrought specimens for sport, particularly for shooting birds. Against a moving target the sportsman needed, not sight, but stocks rightly shaped—even the best shotguns of today have scarcely anything you can call a sight on them, and those most skilled in their handling do not try to use the sights. But they do have the barrel so placed that the eye naturally goes along it towards the target. And gradually through centuries this development, implying a certain shape and angle of the stock, occurred in the musket.

A development also occurred in the means of firing. At first it was necessary to have a burning 'match' with which to light the little pinch of powder beside the touch-hole. The act of applying this match upset any attempt to aim. And it was inconvenient to carry a smouldering piece of material about with you; it would always go out at the wrong moment in any shower of rain. If carried in the cap, as it usually was, it might easily set cap and hair on fire. It had to be blown on to get it burning well before it was used; and this might take one or two puffs or might take some time. In spite of all these disadvantages, these muskets lit by matches were in use for a considerable time. They developed into the matchlock, which had a little piece of metal at the side of the weapon to hold the burning match (made out of cotton soaked in saltpetre), and when a trigger was pulled, the burning match was brought into contact with the gunpowder. This permitted more accuracy in aim. Later, in Germany and Spain there appeared the wheel-lock, with a metal wheel at the side of the priming pan. A piece of iron pyrites pressed against this wheel, which had cogs on it. The trigger rotated the wheel, or released a spring to rotate it; the wheel struck sparks from the pyrites. This was too complicated a mechanism to replace the matchlock for ordinary infantry, and the matchlock did not disappear until the flintlock appeared. This is the familiar thing seen in many old sporting weapons: a flint is held above the pan; the action of the trigger and a spring brings this rapidly down against a cover of metal that protects the priming of powder from damp. As the flint pushes this moveable steel pan cover away, the priming powder is exposed to the sparks falling from it.

Gradually during the seventeenth century the flintlocks replaced other types of musket. Percussion caps, which would go off when struck by the hammer of a musket, were invented early in the nineteenth century, but were not used by the British Army for many years after their invention. After a prolonged trial by the Army authorities, they were adopted in 1835. By 1850, British conservatism could no longer resist the development of the rifle, though many of our troops in the Crimean War (1853-56) were still armed with the percussion musket, 'Brown Bess.' No more muskets were made for issue to the British Army after 1855.

The principle of rifling a weapon had been discovered early in the sixteenth century.

The first muskets were more accurate than the arquebus, but not accurate enough. Within the smooth-bored barrel the projectile hopped about as the gases produced by burning the propellant blew past it, now on one side and now on the other. The direction it took when leaving the muzzle was somewhat determined by the direction in which it was hopping at that moment. The lead ball, in later muskets, was covered with a heavy grease or wax or a plaster, so that it would not bounce around so much; but rifling gave a better and more mechanical positioning of the projectile in the grooves cut within the barrel. And a projectile from a rifle flies more accurately because it is made to spin, and like a spinning top keeps itself in the same line.

A rifled musket was even slower to load and fire than an ordinary musket. The bullet had to fit tightly in the grooves of the rifling and it could not be pushed down from the muzzle without a great deal of effort. Ramrods had to be heavier and stouter, and often the bullet had to be forced down by the use of quite a heavy hammer on the end of the ramrod. Therefore, the first rifled muskets were developed for sport and for hunting. The rifle did not come into war until men who kept themselves by hunting, George Washington's Colonials, used it for their sniping. But that is a later story.

The early unrifled muskets could be dangerous at four hundred yards' distance, but a man was most unlucky to be hit at far shorter ranges. They were too inaccurate for the musketeer to be sure of hitting a single man moving even at twenty yards' range. It may seem surprising, when this is considered, that armies remained in the close order natural to them when they carry armour and use shock weapons. Why did not the soldiers of Tudor or Cromwellian times scatter into small units, or even into individual skirmishers, so that they could not be hit by the fire of their opponents—except by accident? The answer to this lies in the fact already emphasised: the slowness of fire of the musket made it necessary for the men with muskets to be protected by men with pikes. No other infantry weapon could hold up a cavalry charge; and the pike could do this only if the pikemen were massed closely together in several ranks.

The complicated motions of loading a musket—about sixty motions were necessary, and at one period over thirty orders—could be carried out most rapidly if men had practised these motions until they were thoroughly accustomed to them. Therefore, drill and the drill-sergeant became of great military importance. Men were, of course, drilled in the actual movements they would carry out in battle; but the drill was more difficult than the keeping in step and in line which was the essence of the drill in Greek or Roman days. The musketeer must not only do his job neatly and quickly; he must also do it in a confined space with the pikes on each side of him. And the pikemen must also be drilled so that they would always present a hedge of metal points from which any cavalry would flinch.

These musketeers, the primitive infantry of our day, were men using a mechanism in battle, and gradually they were drilled and trained to become themselves machines. Victory lay in their imperturbable march forward under fire until they were at so close a range that their clumsy weapons could cause disorder in the enemy line. Safety under enemy attack lay in their holding their fire till the moment when enemy cavalry charging were only a few yards from them, and then as one man firing a volley that would break the enemy charge. During all this period when shock was still of great importance, the best infantry became more and more machine-like, until this man-machinery had been perfected by the greatest of the Prussians, Frederick the Drillmaster.

Cavalry, meanwhile, for some time came to rely less on shock than on a combination of shock and fire. The horse-pistol, the sort of thing Dick Turpin carried, was one of the main weapons used by Cromwell's cavalry, for example. Cavalry could with some safety approach fairly close to an infantry formation, which would naturally hold its fire because it feared that it might be reloading when the cavalry charged. Then horsemen would ride up almost to the pike-points and discharge their clumsy pistols in the faces of the men on foot. The horsemen hoped to put their opponents in disarray or cause some of them to turn tail, when they could be ridden down with swords. Even when Cromwell's cavalry attacked other cavalry, their aim was first to discharge their pistols effectively and then to use their weight and solidity for the shock of the charge.

Discipline was therefore very necessary for the infantry, who without it would have been exposed to cavalry attack. And soon it became useful or essential for a division of function to be made between various ranks or subunits of the musketeers, so that one portion could fire their volley and another portion remain with muskets ready to fire if a cavalry charge occurred. In the sixteenth century two methods of volley firing for musketeers were worked out. No problem had arisen when the musketeers were so few that all of them could be in the front rank with a pike on each side. But this gave too little fire, and as more firearms were made, the musketeers became proportionately more numerous. The first method of volley firing was used for troops advancing. The front rank, as it came within a short distance of the enemy, would fire and then stand fast, allowing the second rank to advance through it and fire a second volley. Soon musketeers were in three ranks, and a third rank would march through the first two to dress, to blow up their matches, to go through all the rigmarole of firing. Meanwhile, the first rank would be reloading, and after a time would be ready to press farther forward and fire another volley.

This tied infantry to a slower rate of advance than had ever been the case before. And the second method, similar to the first but in the reverse direction, adopted for troops on the defensive, was unsatisfactory because the first rank would retire after firing. Such a movement to the rear could become a retreat. It was difficult to have a sort of barn dance going on, with the first rank falling back and the second rank simultaneously advancing to occupy exactly the ground they had held. So various other movements were attempted. At the battle of the Boyne, in 1690, the men in the front rank after firing fell on their faces, allowing the second rank to fire over them. The second rank then knelt down to permit the third to fire. But there was a snag in this: all three ranks had to reload at once, and therefore the system did not work on the defensive. The only time when it worked was when the infantry were going to charge immediately after they had fired their volleys. Even then it was clumsy, for men who were going to charge were lying down or kneeling.

To have spread out all the musketeers in one line would have made them too thin-spread to stand attack by cavalry or by a massed infantry. They could not fire over each other's heads as archers could 'in the ancient and vulgar manner of discipline,' two centuries or more before. Therefore, the first subdivision crept into the drilled homogeneous army: and this subdivision came in the form of volley firing by platoons.

In this method of firing, each battalion was divided into two or four platoons or grand divisions, as they were sometimes called, and the first rank of each of these subunits fired at the word of command, then usually these ranks fell back to reload immediately behind the second rank, which also fired. The whole process, when fully developed at the end of the sixteenth century, went according to this account:

> Let us suppose our Battalion drawn up with the Army on the Field of Battle, three deep; their bayonets fixed on their muzzles, the Grenadiers divided on the Flanks, the Officers ranged in the Front; and the Colonel, or in his absence, the Lieut.-Colonel (who I suppose fights the Battalion) on Foot with his Sword drawn in his Hand, about 8 or 10 paces in their Front, opposite the Centre, with an expert Drum by him. He should appear with a chearful Countenance, never in a Hurry, or by any Means ruffled; and to deliver his Orders with great Calmness and Presence of Mind.
>
> The first Thing the Colonel should do, is to order the Major and Adjutant to divide the Battalion into 4 grand Divisions.
>
> As the Commanding Officer will be exposed to the Fire of his own Men, as well as

that of the Enemy he is to take, special Care that he keep opposite the 2 Centre Platoons while the other Parts of the Battalion keep firing; and he must also take as great Care that when it comes to the Turn of the Centre Platoons to fire, that both he and the Drum step aside and return as soon they have done, otherwise they must fall by their own Fire.

On the word 'March' the Officers move to the Rear of the Intervals. The Senior Captain posts himself in the Centre 8 or 10 paces from the Rear Rank, the other Officers 4 paces from the Rear Rank, dividing the Space. The Ensigns with the Colours in the Centre Rank on the Right and Left of the 2 Centre Platoons; Sergeants on the Flanks and in the Rear between the Officers. The Drums divided in 3 Parts on the Right and Left in Rear of the 2 Centre Platoons, all dressing with the Sergeants. The Major and Adjutant on the Flanks.

The Colonel having thus spoke cheerfully to the Men he then gives the word 'March'; at which Time the Drum beats to the March and when the Battalion has got within 4 or 5 Paces of him, he turn towards the Enemy and marches slowly down till he finds them begin to fire upon him; upon which he orders his Drum to cease beating and turning to the Battalion, gives the word 'Halt!' and then orders his Drum to beat a 'Preparative,' on which the 6 Platoons of the First Firing make ready, etc., etc.

The Officers and Sergeants of these Platoons are to take great Care that the Soldiers

> level well their Arms so that their Fire may have Effect on the Enemy as also caution them to wait the next Signal of Drum. (Here the Men ought in training them to be us'd to that of recovering their Arms sometimes instead of firing, which will make them take in waiting for Orders to fire).
>
> The Platoons being presented, the Colonel orders the Drum to beat a second 'Flam' on which they fire and immediately recover their Arms, fall back and re-load as fast as they can, &c. &c.[1]

At the battle of Dettingen, in 1743, when the British and Hanoverians won a victory over the French, the British infantrymen, using improved muskets, stood facing the French, who were using their artillery and were preparing for a charge. The musketeers advanced to within sixty paces of the enemy and then let them have it. The effect of their fire is described as follows in the diary of an officer of the Royal Welch Fusiliers:

> Our Army gave such shouts before we were engaged, when we were about one hundred paces apart before the action began, that we hear by deserters it brought a pannick amongst them. We attacked the Regiment of Navarre, one of their prime regiments. Our people imitated their predecessors in the last war gloriously, marching in close order, as firm as a wall, and did not fire till we came within

[1] *Kane's Campaigns, 1689-1712,* quoted in Field, *Old Times Under Arms,* pages 91-93.

> sixty paces, and still kept advancing; for, when the smoak blew off a little, instead of being amongst their living we found the dead in heaps by us; and the second fire turn'd them to the right about, and upon a long trot. We engaged two other regiments afterwards, one after the other, who stood but one fire each; and their Blue French Foot Guards made the best of their way without firing a shot. . . .
>
> Our Regiment sustained little loss, tho' much engaged; and indeed our whole army gives us great honour. . . . What preserved us was our keeping close order, and advancing near the enemy ere we fir'd. Several that popp'd at one hundred paces lost more of their men, and did less execution for the French will stand fire at a distance, tho' tis plain they cannot look men in the face.[2]

It will be seen that the musket was still extremely inaccurate, but was seriously effective if fired at a solid mass of enemy troops at a range of less than a hundred yards. By this time almost all the men in the ranks could carry muskets; pikes were no longer necessary. It was still necessary to have a barrier of cold steel against enemy cavalry charging at a moment when too many of the musketeers were reloading their pieces—or more rarely against an enemy infantry charge. But this barrier could now be put up by the musketeers themselves; the bayonet had been invented.

Both pike and musket were heavy and clumsy weapons, and it was not possible for the same man to handle both of

[2] Field, *Echoes of Old Wars.*

them. A musket usually weighed fifteen pounds or more. In 1647, a gentleman named Puységur, who came from the town of Bayonne in southwestern France, was in command of French troops holding Ypres. As seems to be the custom in those parts, he was short of men; he was particularly short of reliable pikemen. And he could get no reserves.

He himself probably carried one of the short daggers with rounded handles which were at that time manufactured in Bayonne. He must have tried one of these daggers jammed into the muzzle of a broken musket, and found that it fitted and made a tolerable substitute for a pike. He sent to Bayonne for a consignment, and when they came, distributed them among his musketeers, who were taught to plug them into the muzzles of their weapons after the weapons had been fired. The daggers were known as 'Bayonnettes.' By 1663, or perhaps a little earlier, English soldiers were using plug-bayonets of this kind.

By 1671, plug-bayonets had been issued to all French fusilier regiments. It was difficult to rely on these bayonets, because they shook loose from the barrels into which they were plugged the first time men lunged with them. Therefore, the plug-bayonet was improved in 1687 by a small socket being cut in the wood of the handle, into which a wedge or plug fitted to keep the whole thing in place. This change introduced by Vauban, was at once adopted by the French Army, and by 1703 the pike had practically been abandoned in France.

It was impossible to fire the musket while a bayonet of the plug or socket type was inserted in its muzzle. In 1689, the troops of William and Mary of England were defeated by Highland forces under Dundee at Killiecrankie, because these troops had their bayonets plugged in too soon when they should have been firing, and then took them out to fire or to reload just before the Highlanders charged. The Highlanders rushed them before they could get the bayonets back into their weapons. It was quite natural that the commander of the defeated force should think up another type of bayonet.

This was the ring-bayonet, which was clipped on to the outside of the musket barrel by a large metal ring. This permitted the musket to be loaded and fired while the bayonet was attached. Infantry could now deliver their fire and charge at once.

The pike was no longer of use, but, as usual, custom retained the old weapon long after its use had gone; far into the eighteenth century the English Army still retained a colour guard of fourteen pikes for every company. And the pike reappeared, to our dismay, in 1941.

Ring-bayonets were in general use for about a hundred years after their invention. Their defect was that they were difficult to fit and became loose if the metal ring stretched in any way. In 1805, Sir John Moore—who at that period was revolutionising the tactics of the British Army—introduced a bayonet that could be fitted rapidly and securely by means of a spring clip—the method in use to this day.

While the fire-power of muskets was increasing during the seventeenth century, because of gradual improvement in the weapons themselves, because of better drill, and because of the invention of the bayonet and the disappearance of the pike, another form of fire-power was at the same time becoming increasingly important. The field gun was becoming more handy and more accurate. It was no longer a cumbrous thing mainly intended for siege purposes, but occasionally used in mobile warfare; a differentiation, or 'division of labour,' was occurring in artillery, so that armies began to have a 'siege train' of heavy guns that were only hauled up from the base for sieges and a 'field train' of lighter pieces for normal fighting.

Gustavus Adolphus, King of Sweden, early in the seventeenth century, won the victories that gave Protestantism the certainty of survival in northern Europe, mainly by skilful use of light field pieces as auxiliary weapons. His great aim was always to keep down the weight of his guns, and one of his favorite weapons was a one-and-a-half-pounder. Guns began to be far more accurately and carefully made; at first some had been made like barrels out of metal staves bound together with rings that were shrunk on to them; later all were made, or almost all, by casting the gun as a solid lump of metal and then boring down the centre of it to make the barrel and chamber. Gustavus Adolphus had some pieces made of leather strongly lined with metal, but even with the poor powder and light charges of those days such weapons can scarcely have been good for more than a few rounds.

The first mobile field pieces were mounted on wagons. They could only be aimed laterally by hauling the wagon around, and they were elevated for range in even more slow and primitive ways. Some had wedges that had to be hammered in on each side of the muzzle to raise the front of the gun. Others had an apparatus rather like the bars used by athletes for a high jump. The cross-bar could be raised or lowered on pegs or notches in the upright bars; and the muzzle of the gun rested on the cross-bar and was raised or lowered with it. There was no recoil mechanism for these guns and no springs on the wagons; so the whole thing used to shake itself to pieces after a number of discharges.

Later field pieces were made with their own wheels and a trail which lay on the ground behind them. The recoil was taken by this trail shifting back along the ground. It was easy to lift the trail and shift it sideways to give lateral aim; but elevation was still given by a clumsy business of wedges until a rough screw arrangement, each turn of the screw filed out by hand, was developed to position the gun.

But the number of field guns, in the sixteenth, seventeenth, and early eighteenth centuries, was still fairly small in proportion to the size of the armies. It will be remembered that the Carthaginians, fighting defensive position warfare for their city, had used one 'engine' or piece of artillery for every hundred soldiers. At Blenheim, in 1704, Marlborough had one piece of field artillery for nine hundred men. Napoleon, at Borodino in 1812, had one gun for every two hundred and forty men. In this great battle at the gates of Moscow there seems to have been the heaviest concentration of fire-power known in the Napoleonic era; the Russians had even more guns than Napoleon and an even higher proportion between guns and man-power. At the battle of Waterloo, as we have already noted, Wellington had about one gun for every four hundred men; Napoleon was better armed with one gun for every three hundred.

But with the Napoleonic era we have entered a new phase of warfare, in which artillery becomes more important than it had been in the previous three hundred years. In those three hundred years guns were only an auxiliary weapon, of increasing importance, but seldom of decisive effect.

Another weapon or arm was developed during this period to do the same job as the gun. This was the *grenade*, so-called because it was compared to a pomegranate. As muskets were inaccurate, and attacking troops had to get within a few yards before they delivered their fire and prepared to charge, it was possible for men to run forward and throw a shell with the fuse burning into the ranks of the enemy. It was a risky job and hard work; the tallest and strongest men were chosen to be grenadiers. Soon there were grenadier companies in each regiment; the use of special units for throwing or bowling these grenades dates from about 1660. By about 1740, the

Russian Army had separate grenadier battalions; but it is hard to determine whether these men were all in fact armed with grenades. The word 'grenadier' was already becoming a title of honour. Napoleon organised whole brigades and divisions of grenadiers; but these were armed like ordinary infantry. Because the tallest and strongest men had been chosen originally to be grenadiers, and because they had been placed in the position of honour 'on the right of the line,' the word grenadier soon became a mere title. Our own Grenadier Guards, formerly the Foot Guards, received their present title after 1815 as an honour for their gallantry at Waterloo. They did not, in becoming grenadiers, alter their arms or tactics.

Grenadier companies, some of which were armed with grenades and some of which had ordinary infantry equipment, but were the 'storm troops' of their units, existed in the British Army until 1858. But when the rifle was replacing the musket, it was no longer possible for whole companies of grenadiers to run up to their enemy's lines and roll, bowl, or pitch their grenades among the legs of their opponents. Riflemen (or even men with good accurate muskets) could pick them off before they got within range. Skirmishers prevented their getting near enough to the main lines of their enemies. The hand-grenade, therefore, began to go out of use during the Napoleonic period, and almost disappeared from warfare for a century, until it was revived by the trench warfare of 1914.

The first phase of modern war, the phase with which we have been dealing, reached its full development with the army of Frederick the Great of Prussia.

Cavalry, by the time of Frederick the Great, had become of relative unimportance in battle. In many campaigns, including some of Frederick's, it was called the decisive arm because its shock tactics, or a combination of shock and fire, actually won the battle after infantry fighting had weakened or loosened the organisation of one of the contending armies. But this infantry fighting was in fact decisive; the cavalry only clinched the argument. And in a few campaigns, such as Cromwell's, cavalry had been without doubt the decisive arm. By the time of Marlborough, cavalry no longer had great value when employing shock and fire; its pistol fire-power was too little, and the fire-power of the infantry armed with musket and bayonet was too great. A cavalry that checked to fire exposed itself to a destructive volley from a section of the infantry it was attacking. Marlborough allowed his cavalry 'but three charges of powder and ball to each man for a campaign, and that only for guarding their horses when at grass, and not to be made use of in action.'[3] But cavalry remained of great value for purely shock action, and after Marlborough had pinned an enemy to his ground by powerful infantry attacks, he launched his cavalry against them to cut their formation to pieces.

Cavalry are large targets; it was the increasing fire-power of the infantry that by Frederick's day had reduced the horse to a subsidiary role—that of pursuit. Yet partly through custom, and partly through the need for shock action by the infantry to complete the work that firepower began, infantry formations remained extremely tight-packed, and Frederick drilled the whole infantry of his army to move almost as one man.

In the three centuries before Frederick there were many developments of warfare that we need scarcely deal with here: the trench systems developed in northern France, the great fortifications of Vauban, the extreme slowness of sieges, the custom of going into winter quarters and of only fighting one campaign a year. From these and other

[3] *Kane's Campaigns,* quoted by Fuller, *Decisive Battles,* page 396.

elements the autocratic monarchies of Europe built up a system of war that Frederick both exemplified and helped to destroy.

The system of slow eighteenth-century warfare derived directly from the political aims of the antagonists and from the social relations between the states and the soldiers they owned. There were few wars in this period that had a national character: war was a continuation of autocratic diplomacy which tried to win a province or a town, at most the succession to a throne, from some opposing but similar autocracy. And the monarchs contending had a very sharp and personal feeling about their own property; willing to grab a town owned by somebody else, they were extremely anxious not to lose any town of their own. They, therefore, spread their armies out in detachments over wide fronts, seldom and slowly concentrated for battle, avoided battle whenever possible, and hoped by siege and manoeuvre against an enemy's communications to secure their limited aims at a very limited cost.

The soldiers of the period were usually conscripted serfs or peasants with remarkably little interest in the wars they were fighting. They had to be kept in camps or barracks for fear they would desert; they could not be trusted to forage for food or other supplies in an enemy countryside. All their supplies had, therefore, to be brought to them from depots in the rear. These depots could not be very far away; roads were very bad, wagons very slow and clumsy. If the depot was a long distance away, a wagon would start out with forage for the horses of the cavalry; but before it got near to the army, the mules or horses dragging the wagon would have eaten all the forage carried in it. When an army moved far, it had, therefore, to establish behind it a number of depots, and its supplies came stage by stage from one depot to another until they reached the fighting forces.

This question of supply has often influenced strategy and tactics to a very great extent. It still does so. But there probably has never been a system of warfare more subject to the overruling mastery of supply than that of the eighteenth century—at least in Europe. In Asia armies had often been cumbered, not only with immense supplies, but also with hundreds of thousands of camp followers. A French writer describes the army of a Mogul Emperor as follows:

> The cavalry forms the principal section, the infantry is not so big as is generally rumoured, unless all the servants and people from the bazaars or markets who follow the army are confused with the real fighting force: for in that case I could well believe that they would be right in putting the number of men in the army accompanying the king alone at 200,000 or 300,000 and sometimes even more—when, for example, it is certain that he will be a long time absent from the principal town. And this will not appear so very astonishing to one who knows the strange encumbrance of tents, kitchens, clothes, furniture, and quite frequently even of women, and consequently also the elephants, camels, oxen, horses, porters, foragers, provision sellers, merchants of all kinds and servitors which these armies carry in their wake; or to one who understands the particular state and government of the country, in the kingdom, from which it follows by a certain necessary consequence that the whole of a capital city like Delhi or Acre lives almost entirely on the army and is therefore obliged to follow the king if he takes to

> the field for any length of time. For these towns are and cannot be anything like a Paris, being properly speaking nothing but military camps, a little better and more conveniently situated than in the open country.[4]

In the eighteenth century, European armies can seldom have taken with them quite so large an 'organisation of supplies.' But in his *History of the Thirty Years' War* Guideby mentions an army of 38,000 fighting men, which was followed by 127,000 women, children, sutlers, cooks, and other camp followers. And one of the French armies which fought against Frederick the Great left behind, when retreating, its officers' 'pommards, perfumes, powdering- and dressing-gowns, bag-wigs, umbrellas, parrots; while a host of whining lacqueys, cooks, friseurs, players, and prostitutes were chased from the town to follow their pampered masters.'[5]

It will be seen that an eighteenth-century army whose communications or depots were threatened had much to lose. And, therefore, for a period war became a slow stalemate of manoeuvre in which eight miles was a good day's march and three towns taken comprised the achievements of a campaign.

Frederick the Great, warring against powerful empires with forces always inferior to those of his opponents, remained to some extent within the rules of this game; but in other and vital directions he had to break up those rules. War was slow, and war was a matter of shock finally,

[4] François Berniel (1625-88), in *Voyage Contenant la Description des Etats du Grand Mogul.*

[5] Campbell: *Frederick the Great, His Court and Times.*

though fire did much to make a decision by shock possible. Frederick determined from the beginning to alter these ways of war. He would produce an army that could move rapidly. He would produce an infantry that could fire rapidly. But he did so by carrying to its logical limit the drill of his day. His men were drilled to march at a quickstep; they were drilled to fire more rapidly than their opponents. Frederick boasted that they could fire three times as fast. He taught his army to deploy with great rapidity, from a column marching along a road to a single line heading to the flank. The armies he fought against deployed very slowly, and the incredible drill-books of the day almost tied them to the ground they stood on. Each unit could perhaps advance or retire; but only with the utmost difficulty and a great expense of time could it face or move obliquely at an angle to its original deployment. Frederick trained his men to face and move in an oblique formation. He also trained them to use their fire-power to the utmost in thin, wide-stretching, linear formations.

By his greater mobility Frederick was able on the field of battle itself to march a wing of his army or even almost his whole army round to the opponent's flank, and then attack it obliquely so that the fire of his men concentrated on and crumpled up point after point along the enemy line. Major-General Fuller writes of him in *Decisive Battles:*

> In his earlier campaigns he relied more on the bayonet than the bullet, but soon discovered his mistake; for in his later battles he did his utmost to develop the power of both his muskets and his cannon. He was the creator of the first true horse-artillery ever formed, a weapon so little thought of that, from 1759 onward for thirty years, the Prussian was the only horse-artillery in Europe. Further still,

> he was a great believer in the howitzer, because the Austrians, acting normally on the defensive, were prone to hold their reserves behind the ridges occupied by their firing lines. Yet, though so clear-sighted as an artillerist, he never grasped the full value of a trained light infantry, and this is all the more astonishing because at the battle of Kolin the Austrian Croats and Pandours were largely responsible for his defeat.[6]

By 'horse-artillery' is meant artillery which is not slowly and clumsily dragged by long teams of horses to the battlefield and unable to move during action from the point where it is deployed, but artillery that can be limbered up and moved quickly, as quickly as the cavalry it accompanies, to a new point as an action develops. Here again Frederick achieved tactical mobility by patient drill and continuous training of his men. For nearly two centuries battle had almost always consisted of a head-on encounter by two armies meeting face to face. Even Marlborough's battles had essentially that character. Frederick brought back again the tactical manoeuvre, the swing to envelopment. And it is symbolic that at one of his most striking victories, at Leuthen, his flank attack jammed the enemy infantry so closely together that, at the vital point of the battlefield, they were thirty to a hundred ranks deep. His own infantry, two or three ranks deep, could use their weapons to the full; this packed mass of Austrians could use only a small proportion of their muskets. Frederick's artillery could not fail to find a target among them. And when towards the end of the battle Frederick's cavalry

[6] *Decisive Battles,* page 451.

drove the Austrian cavalry off the field and attacked the rear of the disordered Austrian infantry, a battle that almost ranks with Cannae had been won.

The army of Frederick the Great, therefore, stands at the end of a long period of development in which the main process has been the creation of a force capable of hitting, increased by fire-power, like a single heavy hammer. But, like most of the great developments of history which sum up a period and carry that period to its highest level, Frederick's army had within it the seeds of a new period. He bought mobility with the old currency of drill; but he bought so much of it that his troops in effect entered the new and revolutionary period when not drill but *élan* would wrench warfare into speed and mobility. Frederick is both the summing-up of the age of the drilled musketeer and at the same time, with his horse-artillery, the precursor of Napoleon the Gunner.

7
Napoleon

Napoleon was a gunner who became emperor. Previous captains, whose mark on the history of war and of mankind can bear mention on the same page with his, had been other sorts of soldiers. Gustavus Adolphus was a king who liked guns; that is very different from being a gunner who likes making kings. The period that we enter with Napoleon is one in which first the marksman-skirmisher and then the gun, the long-range weapon, uncoffin warfare from the winding sheets of the past, restore movement to it, and decision. The gun and the musket that could be aimed so revolutionise war that the process of change takes on its own momentum, and goes far beyond Napoleon's own innovations, even beyond his understanding.

The political and economic processes that produced the French Revolution, and made possible Napoleon as its heir and as its executioner, are not our concern in these pages. But everyone knows that the Industrial Revolution was producing, during the years before the French Revolution, an age of iron, of simple machinery, of mechanical power. This age opens with the American War of Independence, the formation of the state that was later, in our own days, to carry mechanical power to its highest level of development. And the weapons and tactics of the Napoleonic period first begin to show their shape, symbolically enough, at the place now called Pittsburgh. English troops, with their auxiliaries, colonial militiamen—of whom a George Washington was the officer—there met and were massacred by French troops whose auxiliaries were red Indians. The Indian way of fighting was entirely primitive; it would not have seemed out of place to some of the soldiers of the army of the Great King invading Greece from Persia in 480 b.c. They fought by arrow and by ambush; they knew nothing of drill, but much of cover. The best-trained troops were useless against them if those troops knew nothing beyond the conventionalised formalities of a European battlefield. In the clash between drilled regiments and the tribes of 'braves,' war returned—as all arts must sometimes do—to the primitive; conventions built up by centuries were broken down, so that a new convention, embodying the powers of new instruments and new powers of old instruments, could emerge.

The British Army needed to produce soldiers who could meet the Indian allies of the French on equal terms; this need led to the formation of our Royal American Rifles, the first modern infantry. These forerunners of the rifle brigade wore a uniform designed to hide the man wearing it. All previous uniforms, from the liveries of royal guards or noblemen's retinues, through the red coats of Cromwell's troops, to the elaborate and desperately uncomfortable kit of George the Third's infantry, had been designed largely to make the wearers obvious. In battles that were like large and brutal games in the open fields, commanders and men needed to know who was on their side and who was against them. The uniforms they wore were, therefore, brightly coloured, like the jerseys worn by football teams. They were also often elaborate, even decorative, partly because it was considered good for drilling men into automata to make them slave at polishing buttons and other gear; partly because the richness of uniform showed the wealth and therefore the fighting resources of the autocrat at whose service was the man within the uniform. Uniform of this sort was a hopeless handicap in the forests of America. The Rifles, therefore, wore green jackets. And they wore black buttons, as their inheritors do to this day.

From the disaster at Pittsburgh (then Fort Duquesne) George Washington was the only officer on the English side to escape alive. Some years later he began to teach himself and the British Army, on a larger scale than could derive from one scrambled ambush, the possibilities of the new tactics. These possibilities largely arose from the fact that an accurate long-range weapon now existed. The musket, and in particular the rifled musket, had ceased to be a weapon valuable only at a hundred yards or so against a mass of troops. It could be used against a single man, even against a man partially under cover. It could be used at ranges so great that the man using it could often reload before his opponent could rush him.

This is an extremely important development. I have already described how, with ancient muskets that were slow and clumsy and inaccurate, infantry had to keep in close order; if they did not do so, they would be ridden down by cavalry or charged by the opposing infantry when reloading and helpless. But as reloading came to need less time, and as it became more and more dangerous to approach within some hundreds of yards of an infantry trained to aim, there obviously had to come a period when this need was relaxed and some part of any infantry formation, or perhaps the whole of it, could operate in open order, relying on its fire-power and its power to move to protect itself against enemy action. This period had been reached before 1776, when Washington's straggling militia and half-starved 'Continentals' faced good British and German troops and to the world's surprise dealt harshly with them.

For generations, even perhaps for centuries, it had been of advantage to a body of infantry that when the forces were in close contact the enemy should fire first. 'Gentlemen of the Guard, fire first!' was not a mere courtesy; there was solid advantage to be gained from it. In the thick smoke of the enemy's volley, and while his men were reloading, you could go forward to fire and then to charge. But now the enemy, if treated in this courteous and conventional manner, was able to open fire from a considerable distance and repeat his fire before you could get at him. Soon it was of great advantage to get in your shot first. And, therefore, soon there was room for skirmishers on every battlefield.

But armies have a brittle conservatism which forces innovations to take roundabout routes. Militia or volunteer forces made up hastily from civilians can more easily do the common-sense thing or adopt the obvious tactics. Skirmishing and skirmishers had become technically possible well before the American War of Independence. But such methods and such men were wholeheartedly condemned by all decent soldiers as cowardly and unfair. That they could be effective was proved by the battle on the Plains of Abraham near Quebec, in 1759, when 'a great many of our officers and soldiers were wounded by a body of burghers from Quebec, selected as good marksmen, who lay concealed in a field of corn opposite our right. It was from these skulkers that General Wolfe received both his wounds, as he gave direction in the front of the line.'[1]

These 'skulkers' were soon to be paralleled by others whose fire would not merely kill a general at the moment of his victory, but would defeat whole armies. A British

[1] From the *British Magazine,* March, 1760, quoted by Field, *Echoes of Old Wars.*

officer describes the effect of the guerrilla tactics of the first American colonists to fight, at and near Lexington, as follows:

> The Country at this time took ye Alarm and were immediately in Arms, and had taken their different stations behind Walls, &c, on our Flanks, and thus were we harassed in our Front, Flanks and Rear . . . it not being possible for us to meet a Man otherwise than behind a Bush, Stone hedge or Tree, who immediately gave his fire and off he went.2

It is so natural for the modern infantryman to think in terms of cover that he needs to be reminded that, for hundreds of years, the main engagements between armies took place outside cover, or with cover for only one or two positions held by units of troops. After the battle of Bunker Hill in the American War of Independence, the adjutant of a British Marine Battalion wrote home. 'We killed a number of rebels, but the cover they fought under made their loss less considerable than it would otherwise have been.'[3] It is now generally recognised by historians that this engagement, although technically the British remained masters of the position, was a victory for the Americans, whose fire-power and use of cover caused casualties so heavy that the British force was partially crippled thereby.

Another British officer writing of the same battle said, 'The ground . . . is the strongest I can conceive for the kind of defence the rebels made which is exactly like that

[2] Field, *Echoes of Old Wars,* quoting a letter from Major W. Soutar, of the Marines, April 22, 1775.

[3] *Ibid.*

of the Indians, viz. small enclosures with narrow lanes bounded by stone fences, small heights which command the passes, proper trees to fire from and very rough and marshy ground for the troops to get over.'[4] At a later stage in the campaign, British forces found the normal type of colonial fence to be a very serious military obstacle. These fences were made by men clearing the ground of trees, and consisted of tree-trunks piled in an open zigzag so that the ends locked. Thus, at the beginning of open-order infantry fighting, we find the first development, not only of cover, but of the use of field fortifications covering most of the front of an army in actual battle. For some centuries field fortifications had covered much of the front of armies extended in cordons through the Low Countries, the cockpit of Europe. But these armies had usually come to fight outside their entrenchments and battle had occurred only when, by piercing a line or moving to a flank, the opponent could be caught without protection. Now we enter a period when the fence-fortifications of the battle of Monmouth changed gradually into Lee's breastworks in the battles of the Wilderness of Virginia and finally into the trenches of 1914-18.

Washington's army contained several units, such as Morgan's Rifles, which consisted largely of men who had earned their living by hunting. They carried 'squirrel guns,' weapons accurate enough to shoot a squirrel. They made ideal skirmishers; and their independence and initiative were as important as the weapons they carried. They required no drillmasters; it was not necessary for the drums to beat a 'flam' before they fired. Their rifled weapons were incomparably better than the Tower muskets of the British; even the ordinary American muskets

[4] *Ibid.*

were better than this old weapon, which could seldom hit at forty yards or more. For instance, the yellow flints in the British muskets were good for only fifteen rounds, the American black flints were good for sixty rounds.

Washington's army was not made up only of skirmishers and militia. Out of his own relatively long-service soldiers he hammered regular units of the line capable of the concentrated volley fire and the shock action and the coordinated close-order movement that would enable them to act as a solid striking force.

When a new tendency appears in human history, it often begins by showing in miniature almost all the tendencies that will matter in the development of the next period of the future. Thus, here at the beginning of modern long-range fighting, we have the skirmishing, the fight by fire from open order, the use of cover, the use of field fortifications covering most of the front of an army in action, accurate rifle fire, and—most important of all—an example of close combination between a regular striking force of well-trained troops and the efforts of a militia little more than an armed population in quality. I have emphasised the value in this war, and the effect on future wars, of these 'skulkers' whose fire largely destroyed British power in America. But it is necessary also to emphasise that, with this type of soldier only, Washington could do little; the British were able to occupy Philadelphia and Washington's force was condemned to the heart-breaking miseries of Valley Forge. He needed, in addition to his skirmishers and riflemen, a force capable of standing up to hammering. He made this force partly by employing a Prussian drillmaster, von Steuben, trained in the schools of Frederick the Great, and partly by gaining the direct assistance of good French troops.

All the same, it was not a Prussian-drilled or French royalist force that drove the English and Hanoverian soldiers out of the United States; it was a force that combined the drill technique of Europe with something new. And the French officers who came back from America were the first to introduce into Europe what had been learned there about skirmishing.

In the American War of Independence, then, were almost all the factors of the Napoleonic period of warfare. But one essential factor was missing: the field gun. Few guns were used on either side, and they had little decisive tactical importance. Napoleon's remaking of warfare, on the other hand, consisted essentially of a fuller development of the new elements in war that had been displayed in America and in the addition to these a new use of fire, particularly of artillery fire, to open the way for decisive manoeuvre.

Two facts reveal the coming of the Napoleonic change in war. One is that the decisive battle of Valmy, in which the French Revolution at its weakest and least prepared defeated the most dangerous threat to its existence, was in the ordinary sense of the word scarcely a battle at all; it was a cannonade. Infantry and cavalry scarcely made contact at effective ranges; artillery did so, and decided the issue. The second fact, of perhaps lesser importance but very revealing, is that Napoleon himself achieved power in France partly by the use, and more by the threatened use, of his own political formula: 'a whiff of grapeshot' in the Paris streets. There have been plenty of cases of captains or generals seizing power by the threat of action by the troops they commanded. Napoleon was the first, I think, to win power by something that was becoming more important than the command of legions—the command of a new technical instrument, artillery.

Napoleon had not the smallest interest in tactics. That may seem a sweeping statement to make about a great captain who revolutionised warfare. But it shows in all his work, in his battles as well as in his writings. It is proved by the fact that the French tactical regulations, the *Règlements d'Infanterie,* drawn up under the monarchy in 1791, were never altered by Napoleon. As First Consul or Emperor he altered almost everything else: the law of property, the division of France into *départements,* all sorts of civilian things. He never altered the regulations for the training and use of his troops. They survived until the reign of Louis Philippe, many years after Waterloo. Oman comments:

> This is all the more strange because that compilation [the *Règlements*] was singularly deficient in the section dealing with skirmishing and the use of light troops. It had the three-deep Frederician line and the column or companies or divisions as its base, and knew nothing of the attack by dense swarms of *tirailleurs* (skirmishers) which had been the salvation of France in 1793.[5]

Napoleon did not need to worry about tactics. He had ready to his hand the new tactical instrument formed by two tendencies: recognition of the value of skirmishing by all technically progressive officers, on whom the American war had impressed this main lesson, and the Revolutionary heavy column determined to break through the enemy. To these two main factors he added, in the form that we shall see, the new powers of artillery.

During the eighteenth century, with the improvement of the musket, fire became so important an element in battle that all infantry was normally drawn up in the

[5] Oman, *Studies in the Napoleonic Wars,* page 91.

formations most suitable for fire: long lines of men three or four deep. Shock still entered into battle, but fire had become so important that tactical formations were designed first for fire and only secondarily for shock. The essence of the change brought about by the French Revolution and Napoleon can be considered as this: a division of labour began, under which fire was carried out by skirmishers in extended order and by concentrated artillery, while shock was carried out by columns of troops disposed in the most suitable order for shock—roughly a square mass rather than a thin line. This division of labour developed out of the inescapable needs of the French Revolution: with disorganised and ragged armies, raised hastily and scarcely trained, it had to face a world armed against it. These armies could not stand in line, were not drilled for the meticulous tactics of Frederick and his successors. They had courage, however, and they had numbers. They had courage from their beliefs, and numbers from the levy *en masse*. The Revolution swept aside all barriers to the production of arms: men swarmed into the workshops demanding the right to make the instruments of war; those controlling these workshops were often forced to open them to public inspection, or even to put the forges out in the Paris streets, to satisfy the public that they were doing everything possible to make the necessary weapons. With these weapons the Revolution armed two or three times the numbers of the armies threatening Paris. Oman writes:

> The new tactics of the Revolutionary army were evolved from a consciousness of superiority in this respect [numbers], a determination to swamp troops that manoeuvred better than themselves by hurling preponderant masses of them, regardless of the loss that must necessarily be suffered.

And Oman defines the tactical system of these armies, which in its most developed form was taken over by Napoleon, as follows:

> It consisted in throwing at the hostile front a very thick skirmishing line, which sheltered and concealed a row of columns of the heaviest sort. The idea was the first line of *tirailleurs* would so engage the enemy and keep him occupied, that the supporting columns would get up to striking distance with practically no loss, and could be hurled, while still intact, upon the hostile first line, which they would pierce by their mere impetus and weight, since they were only exposed to fire for a very few minutes, and could endure the loss suffered in that short time without losing their *élan* or their pace. The essential part of this system was the enormously thick and powerful skirmishing line. Whole battalions were dispersed in chains of *tirailleurs,* who frankly abandoned any attempt at ordered movement, took refuge behind cover of all sorts, but were so numerous that they could always drive in the very thin skirmishing line of the enemy, and get closely engaged with his whole front. The orderly battalion fire of the Austrian or other allied troops opposed to them did comparatively little harm to these swarms, who were taking cover as much, as possible and presented no close body or solid mark for the volley poured at them. There is a very clear description of such a fight in Ditfurth's narrative of the battle of Honderschoote, where Walmoden's Hanoverians, covering the Duke

> of York's flank, fought for four hours against a swarm of *tirailleurs,* who always gave way and took refuge in hedges or buildings when attacked by the bayonet, but always came back to molest the defensive line opposed to them, till after clearing their front eleven times the Hanoverians had to give way in the end, because their original three-deep line had simply been shot to pieces, and about a third of their men had fallen.[6]

The tactical system of the French Revolutionary armies, based on their needs and moral qualities, led to another change that had strategic results. These armies moved as men hurrying: they had no very strict order to keep and they did not march in step. (Normal French infantry, to this day, straggles out of step most of the time.) But the speed of their march, into action and during action, was the quickstep of a hundred and twenty paces to the minute. The armies they fought against maintained the normal barrack-square drill step of seventy paces to the minute. The quickstep is quite natural to a division hurrying: the slow march, as Home Guards have found in Britain, requires long practice. The old armies marched slowly because only when marching slowly can a perfect line be maintained, in spite of any irregularity in the ground. The new French army marched swiftly because its columns, unable to fire much themselves from their narrow frontage, needed and wanted to get swiftly through the field of fire and pierce and overthrow the enemy lines. This, with another factor, gave Napoleon's armies their strategic and tactical mobility.

[6] *Ibid.*

The chaotic supply system [writes Liddell Hart] and the undisciplined nature of the Revolutionary armies compelled a reversion to the old practice of 'living on the country.' And the distribution of the army in divisions meant that this practice detracted less from the army's effectiveness than in the old days. Where, formerly, the fractions had to be collected before they could carry out an operation, now they could be serving a military purpose while feeding themselves.

Moreover, the effect of 'moving light' was to accelerate their mobility, and enable them to move freely in mountainous or forest country. Similarly, the very fact that they were unable to depend on magazines and supply-trains for food and equipment lent impetus to hungry and ill-clad troops in descending upon the rear of an enemy who had, and depended on, such direct forms of supply.[7]

The distribution of the army into divisions, mentioned in the preceding quotations, was another development of the period before his own that Napoleon brought to its full development. The armies of the past had often been subdivided, but subdivided into the troops—or at an earlier period, the personal followers—of each subordinate commander. Each of these subdivisions was likely to consist of infantry or cavalry, who might or might not have some guns with them. Only in the case of separate armies joining, as when Eugene and Marlborough joined, would each of the subdivisions of the army be likely to have infantry, cavalry, and artillery 'belonging to it' in a useful proportion. But the formation of army corps, which began before the French Revolution, altered all this. These corps were real little armies 'on their own.' Each had its own infantry, its own cavalry for protection and reconnaissance

[7] Liddell Hart, *The Strategy of Indirect Approach*, page 122.

and pursuit, its own guns and services. Each could act apart from the other corps that made up the army.

This was in its inception a development of the straggling 'cordon' system of war along the French frontiers and in the Low Countries, when the eighteenth-century generals spread their armies out in wide detachments. Naturally each detachment needed if possible to be self-contained. But it had no considerable influence on warfare until Carnot, the military leader of the French Revolution, began to organise these separate divisions in such a way that while operating separately each could, if need be, support others, or all could, if need be, concentrate at one point for decisive action. Napoleon developed this idea and expressed it in his famous slogan: 'March separately, strike together.'

The division of armies into self-contained units of this sort, and the weaving of these units into cooperative dependence on each other, had at first strategic importance rather than tactical. It mattered in bringing troops to battle rather than in their behaviour on the field of battle. But in Napoleon's hands, while maintaining the utmost strategical importance, it also acquired a tactical value. His 'divisions,' separated in time and space, would be so concentrated for battle that they came, not only against the enemy's front, but also by the very direction of their march against the enemy's flank or rear. And Napoleon developed also a new variant of the old idea of 'fixing and hitting'; he had often, if not always, a corps capable of independent action which acted in time or space as his advance guard; it was the first to engage the enemy and pin down the enemy's main forces, and it enabled Napoleon to bring his other units to decisive attack against an enemy whose forces were known in strength and position. This 'grand advance guard' did not always go in front of Napoleon's other forces; it might be on a flank, and it was always the corps against which the enemy was likely to take action first.

This development of the army into four or five separate corps moving each a day's march or so away from the next, and so arranged in square or lozenge formation that concentration was possible upon any of them that might encounter heavy enemy forces, belongs more to the sphere of strategy than to that of tactics. But it combines with another factor in Napoleon's technique to influence the tactics employed. He needed quick and complete victories. It was not enough for him to outmanoeuvre an opponent and force that opponent to fall back, or to meet the opponent in simple head-on clash from which the defeated army could withdraw in good order. Napoleon had often to fight campaigns in which the number of men at his disposal was considerably less than that of his opponents. He would concentrate his corps on a section of his opponents' forces in such a way as to have, normally, superiority on the field of battle. But if he had then indulged in what might be called 1916 tactics, a long laborious fire-fight, a gradual attrition of the opponents' force, and then an assault over a wide front, his superiority on the field of battle would have disappeared before decision came. The opponent would have reinforced the section of his army engaged, from detachments scattered elsewhere. This need for speedy decision is one of the reasons for the Napoleonic retention of fairly heavy columns in attack. The strategical method imposed the tactical method on him.

I have found that young soldiers are sometimes misled by the use of the word 'column' to describe the Napoleonic formation in attack. These young soldiers think of a column as they themselves know it: a long winding snake of men moving forward three or four abreast. Or, if more modern, and mechanised, they think of a column of vehicles strung out one behind the other, a column of tanks behaving as if they were ships at sea. Actually the Napoleonic column was exactly parallel to the phalanx. A normal battalion in the column formation used for attack would have a frontage of thirty men and a depth of thirty. Only the first two ranks of these men could use their muskets—sixty out of nine hundred. This battering-ram of men depended very little on its own fire-power; it depended for most of its effect on shock. And the preparation by fire for its shock action was carried out by the skirmishing company of each battalion, one-tenth of the strength, and by artillery.

Naturally, when marching, Napoleon's troops moved three or four or six abreast, according to the width of road available. And even when fighting they did not always move in the square columns described. They were given quite often a formation called *ordre mixte,* consisting of alternate battalions in column and in extended line, three deep. This formation permitted far more fire-power, and was used fairly often by troops playing a defensive part in the battle.

The normal formation of the British infantry at the beginning of the Napoleonic Wars was the same as that of the infantry of Frederick the Great: a line of men three deep. The third rank could not fire their muskets with safety to the ranks in front of them. And there were no skirmishers, or very few, ahead of this line during action. When fighting in this formation, British troops had few successes; and it was not until Wellington developed his characteristic linear tactics that the British infantry began to show a superiority over their opponents.

After the war in America the authorities in London had, of course, not only disregarded its lessons, but disbanded the formations of light troops, rangers and rifles, with which the British generals in America had tried to cope with Washington's marksmen. Luckily the British

Army possessed a really progressive soldier to train the new bodies of light infantry necessary. This soldier, Sir John Moore, not only broke with tradition in regard to uniform and drill; he also insisted on men being taught by patient explanation of the reasons for what they were supposed to do. He saw that skirmishers and riflemen could not be expected to fight well under arbitrary discipline, doing things by drilled habit rather than by understanding. He formed light units so powerful and so well instructed that Wellington was always able to put in front of his main line a heavier array of skirmishers than that covering the French columns[8] attacking him. Oman writes of Wellington that his experiences in Flanders in 1794 had taught him that the line cannot contend at advantage with a preponderant mass of light troops, which yield when charged, but return the moment that the charge is stopped. The device which he had thought out to provide against this danger was that he would always make his own skirmishing screen stronger than that of the enemy.

Here, then, is a very simple pattern of part of the development of war. The armies of the French Revolution and of Napoleon win their victories partly because they have a strong screen of skirmishers and are fighting against troops which have a weak screen or none at all. Then later Wellington's army develops a screen of skirmishers heavier than that of the Napoleonic armies, and fairly generally succeeds in defeating them. The matter was not, of course, as simple as all this. But we can say that infantry in open order (skirmishers) was continually becoming of increasing importance as compared with infantry in close order.

[8] Oman, *Studies in the Napoleonic Wars.*

Wellington did not hesitate to break up battalions or larger units and scatter their companies through his army as light troops. And he trained a large proportion of the Portuguese put under his command as light battalions and companies for the skirmishing lines of his divisions. An Anglo-Portuguese division of eleven battalions would have no less than eighteen companies of skirmishers ahead of it; a French division of the same size would have only eleven. In other words, the British Army met the new tactics of the French partly by retaining what was good in previous tactics—the firing-power of the line as compared with the inability of the column to use more than a few of its weapons—and partly by going one better than the French in the development of troops fighting in open order.

But the French armies had another, and, according to the argument I am pursuing, an even more important development of tactics which helped to give them victory from one end of Europe to another. Napoleon phrased this development with a clarity that does not mark all his statements on war: 'Même en plaine les colonnes n'enfoncent les lignes qu'autant qu'elles sont appuyées par le feu d'une artillerie très supérieure, qui prépare l'attaque.' (Even in flat and open country columns cannot break through lines except to the extent that they are supported by the fire of a very superior artillery, which prepares the attack.) These were Napoleon's words to Foy, reported in the latter's memoirs. They embody a truth about warfare that remained a truth until at least 1917.

The student of warfare will not find it necessary for me to emphasise Napoleon's increasing preoccupation with concentrated artillery power. For the civilian, who may not have realised how much Napoleon was a gunner, it may be worth suggesting that Tolstoy's *War and Peace* should be read again. His description of Borodino, the victory that Napoleon won at the point where Hitler in

1941 failed to win, is of the most convincing accuracy. And it shows the Emperor placing and giving orders to his artillery before he deploys or launches any of his troops. This was not a mere question of time, of doing one thing which comes first in time before the next which necessarily comes later. It was Napoleon's constant preoccupation, as he learned more of war from experience, to see that his attacks were covered by so heavy a bombardment that the enemy were shaken or even half-broken at the one vital point on the battlefield where decision could be obtained. And his strategic insight was such that he chose this point with an unerring logic, either at the beginning of the battle or as soon as he had found out by fighting where was the weak link in the enemy organisation. He massed his guns against the weak link, pushing them forward boldly, sometimes well ahead of his infantry; and in these guns he used a high proportion of grapeshot or case-shot. This consisted of many bullets or shot which scattered out of the mouth of the gun to form a deadly pattern.

Wellington had an answer to the French tactics of concentrated artillery fire. He could not answer it by a parallel concentration, for he was seldom given the guns. No one in England had as much insight on this matter as Sir John Moore had possessed on the parallel need for skirmishers. It is significant, for example, that when Wellington for the first and last time met Napoleon in battle, at Waterloo, the British general had a few hundred more infantry than the French Emperor; but he had only one hundred and fifty-six guns against Napoleon's two hundred and forty-six. So Wellington developed another way of meeting the French attack: instead of going one better along the same lines, he hid his troops from artillery fire. By doing so he opened a new era in the tactical handling of infantry.

All through the past of warfare it had been natural for generals to choose, when they could, a position for their armies from which the ground sloped down towards the enemy. They had in this way the upper hand; in any charge or shock action their troops would have the advantage of moving downhill. The enemy climbing towards them were physically exhausted by the effort of climbing before they came to action. In these old battles, when no long-range weapon could damage troops exposed to view, there was no reason to hide an army or any considerable part of it; indeed, most commanders liked to display all their forces in order to overawe the enemy. But now a long-range weapon was becoming of great importance. Wellington avoided its power by choosing positions behind or beyond a rise of ground, in such a way that his troops, often kept lying down until the moment of action, were hidden from view and therefore from fire. This gave him not only tactical security against one of the most powerful factors in the French attack; it also gave him the chance for tactical surprise. The French generals could seldom find out exactly where his line extended. In several battles they pushed their columns forward on a flank in the belief that they were outflanking him; his hidden line was beyond them and took their columns from both flanks.

> It was only when absolute necessity compelled, owing to no cover being available in some parts of the line, that Wellington occasionally left troops in his battle-front visible to the enemy, and exposed to distant artillery fire. The best-known instance of this was the case of his centre brigades at Talavera, which were unmasked perforce, because between the stony hill, which protected his left, and the olive groves, which covered his right, there were many hundred yards of open ground without even a serviceable dip or undulation

> in which the line could be concealed. And this was almost the only battle in which we find record of his troops having suffered heavily by artillery fire before the clash of conflict began.[9]

These words, by the great historian to whom I owe so much of my material on the Middle Ages and on the Napoleonic period, explain his judgment that, against English troops handled in Wellington's way, 'it was the French tactical formation which made [a French] victory impossible.'

Strategically, and on a world scale, Napoleon was a far greater soldier than Wellington. But Wellington was far more than 'the full stop at the end of the chapter,' as he has been called by an English historian. He provided, on the scale of tactics, the two answers to the system of warfare introduced by the American and French Revolutions, the system brought to world-shaking development by the strategic and political genius of Napoleon. And he played his part in carrying war to an even higher stage of development, a stage that Napoleon could not understand. This stage consists essentially of a combination between a well-trained regular striking force and an active armed population. Napoleon came up against this new level of warfare to some extent in Russia, and to some extent in Germany, where serfs were freed and far-reaching reforms carried out in order to form an army, and a Landsturm or Home Guard, that would be national in character rather than servile. But it was in Spain that Napoleon met the full force of this new level of warfare. And it is correct that the word describing the methods of fighting of the armed population should be a Spanish word, *guerrila,* 'little war.'

[9] Oman, *Studies in the Napoleonic Wars,* page 101.

Guerrilla warfare is all skirmishing. It is all 'Indian fighting.' It combines the most primitive methods and tactics with the new factor that during the Napoleonic period is helping to revolutionise war: the individual weapon accurate enough to hit an enemy individual before that enemy sees the man who is handling the weapon. The 'Spanish ulcer' that drained the strength of Napoleon's empire consisted, technically and tactically, of the new way of fighting developed first in America, then by the French Revolutionary armies, then by Wellington, detached from the old way of fighting: guerrillas are skirmishers operating 'on their own' away from—yet in necessary combination with—the regular striking force. The individual fighting man, no longer subject to drilled movement in action and no longer controllable immediately and at all times by a superior, takes his place in decisive action, not only as an auxiliary fighting a few hundred yards ahead of the main body of the army, but also as an auxiliary operating many miles away, against the weakest part of the enemy's organisation, his lines of communication. This is an essential factor in modern warfare that we shall see disappear and reappear.

Tactics, from the development of the musket and bayonet to the armies of Frederick the Great, had mainly followed the line of making a strong disciplined body of drilled infantry whose fire-power and shock-power depended on their automatic obedience. Napoleon recognised the change that came with his own era when he said to Jomini, 'I do not love armies of automatons, I require soldiers to be intelligent.' It was still possible for a single man, if he was Napoleon, to make all the strategical and most of the tactical decisions necessary governing the movements into action and during action of armies of decisive size. Napoleon did this; his chief-of-staff was a mere secretary formulating and distributing his orders.

But when the process of splitting up armies passed, from a formal organisation into army corps or divisions, into the more radical division of labour between striking force and guerrillas, Napoleon and his marshals no longer had a method of command and control suitable for this new shape of warfare. The history of the Peninsular War is in essence a history of the French army dispersing to destroy guerrillas and then being struck when dispersed, or threatened, by the regular forces of Moore and Wellington. As soon as these French armies concentrated to check or throw back the British striking forces, the guerrillas rose again and forced them to a new dispersal. This was a form of war to which the Napoleonic system could find no effective answer.

In Frederick's day the main process of battle had been preparation by musket fire, with some assistance from artillery, and then assault in line with the bayonet. In Napoleon's era the main process of battle was preparation by concentrated artillery fire, with some assistance by skirmishers and other musket fire, and assault in column with the bayonet. But towards the end of Napoleon's day there came these new developments that he could not meet: Wellington's concealment of his main body behind strengthened skirmishers and natural cover, and the guerrillas' concealment in every patch of difficult country on territory lightly held across his flanks and rear. The day of invisible armies had begun, the period symbolised for us by the medieval complaint that knights should fall 'almost without seeing the men who slew them.' Industry was producing weapons of such range and accuracy that armies were beginning to hide themselves in defence and to attack swiftly, by surprise or stealth, or behind a cover of gun-fire and skirmishers, so that the attacking troops should be exposed to fire for the briefest possible time.

All weapons and tactics have been changed since Napoleon's day; but many of the tendencies in war that first developed in those days continue into the present.

8
Machine-Gun and Trench

A striking phrase occurs in one of the histories of the American Civil War. Describing a manoeuvre by Grant, and Lee's counter to it, the historian writes: 'Lee manoeuvred his fortifications . . .'

The history of tactics during the period after Napoleon is partly the history of the development of fire-power, which at first loosens and speeds up warfare and later ties it down to relative immobility; it is partly the history of the development of field fortifications, which reach their full development in the Hindenburg Line of 1917 and are brought to useless perfection in the Maginot Line of 1939. But whereas the development of weapons can be shown as a rising curve on a graph, the development of fortifications for a field army came to their limit in one form, then almost disappeared, to reappear later in another form.

In the previous chapter we mentioned Washington's use of the heavy-timbered colonial fences as breastworks. During the American Civil War the decisive area between the two capitals was so heavily wooded that breastworks of tree-trunks could be constructed along almost any position chosen for defence. Lee, whose army during the decisive campaign was on the defensive, made continual and increasing use of such breastworks; and Grant's artillery was never of sufficient power to breach these field fortifications effectively. They, therefore, had to be assaulted, and battle became largely the question of the power to storm or to assault some 'Bloody Angle' of logs behind which the defenders were sheltered from musket and from rifle fire. Assault had become more difficult by the time of the American Civil War than it had been in the Napoleonic period. It was more difficult for the attacking army to push its field guns forward, in front of its infantry, before the assault began, and to use these guns at relatively short range to smash a hole in the enemy's formation. Sniping and skirmishing by men armed either with rifles or with accurate muskets killed so many gunners that they could not remain exposed to enemy view in front of their own main line of infantry; they had to take position behind it. The distance to be covered by assaulting infantry under fire had increased with the increased range of weapons. And finally, and most important, the greater speed with which small arms could be loaded and fired made it certain that defending troops could still hold their positions with fire, not with bayonets, even when the assaulting troops had got close up to them. The bayonet, the last shock weapon left in warfare, was ceasing to have actual fighting value. General John B. Gordon of the Confederate Army wrote in his *Reminiscences of the Civil War:*

> Very few bayonets of any kind were actually used in battle. . . . The day of the bayonet is passed except for use in hollow squares, or in resisting cavalry charges, or as an implement for constructing light and temporary fortifications.

It was becoming increasingly impossible for formed bodies of troops in close order to charge across the field of fire separating armies and reach the enemy's position while still in sufficiently close formation to use a shock weapon. This was not a question of morale or discipline; at battles such as Gettysburg or those of the Wilderness campaign troops continued to advance after receiving very heavy casualties. But it was physically impossible for them to advance in close-ordered line or column; the enemy's fire destroyed these formations and reduced them to straggling groups of skirmishers capable of fire action, but not of shock action. Lee's field fortifications, wooden breastworks of sufficient height to be an obstacle to men charging, fulfilled two functions: they gave shelter to the defending forces and they physically checked the attackers at points where the defenders' fire could wipe them out while they were checked. Ordinary trenches do not fulfil both these functions; they give shelter from fire, but do not provide a physical obstacle to the assault. It was not until modern industry had so developed that thousands of miles of barbed wire could be coiled in front of the trenches that field fortifications became again of such importance that assault against them was a matter of the utmost difficulty. Between these two periods, that of the breastwork and that of the wired trench, lies a gap in which field fortifications were of lesser importance, though they bulked largely in the Crimean War. And few soldiers were willing to recognise the decrease in value of the bayonet or the fact that men in close order could no longer move under fire.

The difficulty of assault, of a charge by unarmoured foot-soldiers against the fire of precision weapons, was hidden from most students of warfare by a myth and by a reality misunderstood. The myth was that of 'cold steel'; faced by the increasing complexity of modern weapons and tactics, conservative commanders retreated morally and mentally to the shock weapon that they could understand, that seemed both 'safe' and heroic, and was intimately connected with the social myth by which the military castes in Europe maintained their political power and economic security. This social myth, gradually developed over a considerable period, included the proposition that courage, discipline, and will power of peculiar and exclusive sorts had to be possessed by the officers leading troops in modern battle; the need to cultivate these qualities during a whole lifetime was the justification for maintaining an exclusive caste of professional officers. This myth came to pieces during most real wars; the American Civil War was largely fought by 'civilian' leaders, and the French fought best in the war of 1870 when their emperor and generals had surrendered. But the myth was sedulously rebuilt during the periods between wars; in Britain it even survived to quite a large extent the successes of unprofessional Boer farmers and even outlasted the war of 1914-18 in which officers who had not been professional soldiers had perforce to be used (after the first year) for most of the actual fighting, while officers who had been professional soldiers were to a considerable extent—often against their will—translated to the unheroic position of command from a considerable distance in rear. This myth preserved the bayonet, as it preserved the purely decorative sword and lance, because these officer castes felt that the bayonet charge was their special accomplishment that no civilian force was likely to attempt.

A misunderstood fact also kept the idea of the bayonet alive. The fact was that the Prussian Army in six weeks of ceaseless advance had scored decisive victory in 1870. Soldiers admiring this feat of arms misunderstood the essence of the Prussian tactics. Although Colonel Henderson wrote in his *Science of War* (1905) that 'the Germans relied on fire, and on fire alone, to beat down the enemy's resistance; the final charge was a secondary consideration altogether'—in spite of this plain statement by the best military theoretician in Britain at that time, the British and other armies continued to believe that the Germans had won their victory by a fire-fight leading up to assault. They ignored entirely an important fact: that all German infantry formations moving forward in action during that war broke up into loose groups of skirmishers, greatly to the dismay of many German officers who insisted that they ought to move forward in close columns of half companies. And they also ignored the fact that the Germans had won this war by the strategic offensive combined with the tactical defensive: German columns pushed forward to threaten flank or rear of French forces in such a way that the French were usually compelled to try to attack and clear the Germans out of these positions. This was the typical shape of the battles up to and including Sedan.

It is difficult to get any serious measure of the value of the bayonet during the Franco-Prussian War, but in the present century casualty statistics have been improved to such an extent that it became possible to judge statistically the relative value of various weapons. In the Russo-Japanese War of 1904 about 2.5 per cent of the total casualties on both sides were caused by spears, swords, and bayonets. In the Great War of 1914-18 bayonet wounds became so rare that no full statistical record of them was kept: they are included among the 1.02 per cent of miscellaneous casualties and accidents. But just before that war the author of this book, like any other Englishman then being taught any form of infantry training, was taught that attack was carried out by advance in extended order, by short rushes when the enemy fire was considerable, by the building up of a firing line and the mastery of the enemy's fire, and then by a bayonet charge, which should be accompanied by loud yells. This, as the basic pattern of infantry attack, was already at that time fifty years out of date.

The development of the machine-gun in the period between the Franco-Prussian War and the War of 1914-18 increased the difficulties of infantry attack and made the defensive, tactically at least, very much the 'strongest form of war.' Fire, as it developed through the centuries, had for a time made tactical movement easier, because its concentration against enemy units exposed in the open, and closely grouped to give good targets, enabled holes to be blown in the enemy's position. But now the effect of fire was reversed. Enemy armies hidden behind cover could weave in front of themselves a web of fire so closely linked that the attacking infantry found it hard to get through. And early in 1915 it began to be generally recognised that machine-gun fire could 'lock the front.'

The development of the machine-gun before 1915 was relatively slow. That development begins for practical purposes in 1882 when an American inventor, who had concentrated on electrical and chemical processes, met in Vienna an American business man whom he had known in the United States. The business man said to the inventor: 'Hang your chemistry and electricity! If you want to make a pile of money, invent something that will enable these Europeans to cut each other's throats with greater facility.' The inventor was Hiram Maxim, and this chance conversation started him working on the development of the first modern machine-gun.

Long before Maxim's time, men had tried to make a machine that would fire projectiles rapidly one after another. When the Spaniards were developing the first good firearms, a Spanish commander mounted a whole row of these firearms on thirty carts, which he put in front of his infantry. This commander, Pedro Navarro, had several men in the carts whose duty it was to fire all the arquebuses at once, by means of a quick-match or fuse that connected all the weapons in each cart.

Later six to ten muskets would be linked together on a single frame, and this frame would be dragged into action on wheels. These clumsy weapons were called 'organs.' because they looked like these musical instruments. A 'rapid-fire gun' of this sort was used in Charleston in the American Civil War.

A more effective gun used in the American Civil War was that invented by Doctor Gatling of Chicago. He had six barrels fixed round a central axis as if they were staves of a cask. The six barrels revolved about the axis; as each barrel came to the top, a cartridge fell into it from a trough. By the time this barrel had come to the bottom of its circular movement, the cartridge had been pushed home and the breech closed. The cartridge was fired and the barrel began to come up again, ejecting the empty cartridge case. This type of gun was later used by the British Army in colonial wars. The barrels were rotated by a man turning a handle at the side of the gun.

Some years earlier, a Belgian officer had invented a machine-gun with twenty-five barrels, each of which could be fired twelve times a minute, throwing out three hundred bullets in a minute. This gun weighed over a ton, and was carried on artillery wheels as if it had been a normal piece of artillery. In the Franco-Prussian War of 1870 the French foolishly tried to use it as if it were a field gun. As it had less than half the range of the Prussian field guns, and as the idea of hiding guns had scarcely been thought of, this French *mitrailleuse* was of very little use; it was usually knocked out by Prussian field artillery shells before it could do much damage to the Prussian infantry.

After the failure of the *mitrailleuse* few soldiers believed in the machine-gun. In 1873, a Swedish banker, Nordenfeldt, took out a patent for a gun rather like the medieval 'organ.' In 1874, an American, Hotchkiss, patented a weapon rather like the Gatling. Little real progress was made by these inventors until a man of quite a different type came on the scene—Basil Zaharoff.

Zaharoff was a salesman for arms, friend of financiers, adviser to war ministers, and before his end the 'mystery man of Europe' and a power as great as that of ministers. Zaharoff was not a mere profiteer. He sold the best weapons. When he had sold them to one country, he then proceeded to sell rather better weapons to a rival country.

It was not, of course, his business to promote wars. But his business flourished when wars happened to promote themselves. And he, rather than Maxim or the other inventors, should receive our thanks for the machine-gun.

He had been selling very light unarmoured torpedo-boats to various governments. It was suggested to him that machine-guns would be good weapons with which to protect larger vessels from these little torpedo-boats. Zaharoff adopted the idea with enthusiasm. It is much more profitable to sell a weapon, and an antidote to that weapon, than it is to sell the weapon alone.

After tests at Portsmouth the British Government bought, for the defence of its warships, several ten-barrelled Gatlings, a five-barrelled Nordenfeldt, and several other types of machine-gun. And Basil Zaharoff received commission on these sales; he also at once received orders from various governments for rather more powerful armoured torpedo-boats, which would not be damaged by the machine-guns that the British Admiralty had bought.

Then came Maxim. As a child of fourteen, when he had first fired an army rifle, he had held it clumsily and the kick of the rifle had bruised his shoulder. He remembered this. He started to make a machine-gun that would employ this kick to do the business of opening the breech, ejecting the cartridge, and pushing a new cartridge into the breech. Then springs would close the breech and the gun would fire again.

In all its principal features the machine-gun he invented is that of 1914 and today. The first gun he made fired ten shots in a second. Soldiers from all over Europe became interested in the gun; the Tsar's army bought it; Kaiser Wilhelm exclaimed: 'This is the only machine-gun.' And Basil Zaharoff adopted it—which was more important than the approval of any war-lord.

Maxim's experiments had been carried out in London. But the British Government was the last to treat machine-guns for land warfare as important. The British Army went to war in 1914 with fewer machine-guns than the Germans had; and Mr. Lloyd George had to override military opposition in order to get large numbers of the guns manufactured.

According to Brigadier-General Baker-Carr, the first commandant of the British Army's machine-gun school in France, many British battalion commanders of the 1914 vintage 'frankly and cordially disliked' machine-guns. He wrote:

> 'What shall I do with the machine-guns to-day, sir?' would be the question frequently asked by the officer in charge of a field day. 'Take the damn things to a flank and hide them!' was the usual reply.

Naturally on manoeuvres, when machine-guns were treated in this way, it was easy to imagine that infantry could get through machine-gun fire and 'close with the enemy'—to use the phrase that still describes, according to the War Office, the duty of British infantry. When battle came, this proved to be no more than a phrase. And when the barbed wire was added to machine-guns, and the trench systems grew into line upon line of muddy ditches, tactics bogged down in futile immobility.

For many years before this, the power of fire had been so clear that many soldiers had realised that frontal attack would be difficult, and had concentrated on teaching the value of flank attack. This teaching culminated in the Schlieffen plan, the scheme by which the mass of the German Army would march round its enemies, through Belgium and along the coast and beyond Paris, always attacking from the flank and always pressing the French forces together, until a new Cannae or a new Leuthen had been achieved. But Schlieffen's plan was watered down by the timid old general kept in charge of the German Army (largely by the operation of the social myth of which I have already written). Von Moltke the Elder had conquered Austria and France in 1866 and 1870; therefore, Von Moltke the Younger had to be allowed to keep nominal control of the German Army in 1914; real control slipped from his nerveless fingers and the Marne ended the Schlieffen plan. Then for a few weeks, wearying of frontal attacks that cost lives, but gave little results, each army sought to outflank the other, until, to the surprise of each, they found that no flanks were left, that the trenched front stretched unbroken from Switzerland to the sea. The defensive power of fire, of wire, and of the spade had ended mobility in war.

It is curious the way in which a new development in warfare can come into being on a small scale and by accident at some critical point and then drop back out of existence for a period. The tactical factor which, many years later, was going to end the stalemate caused by the machine-gun, barbed wire, and trenches showed itself just before this stalemate supervened. That tactical factor is manoeuvre by vehicles. The crisis of the battle of the Marne was marked by the first large-scale manoeuvre by gasoline-driven vehicles known to military history. General Gallieni, commanding the French forces in and around Paris, moved part of these forces onto the flank of General von Kluck's advancing army by commandeering the taxicabs of Paris and other vehicles. More than anything else this manoeuvre decided the Marne, the 'miracle' that saved Paris and probably saved France from defeat in 1914. Yet it was not repeated and could not be repeated when the armies ceased to have flanks; no vehicles were available that could wrest out a flank by main force, by smashing through some part of the enemy's line. And there were not enough gasoline-driven vehicles, in those days before mass production was developed, to make possible long-range manoeuvre based mainly on the gasoline engine.

The soldiers on each side of the trench lines in 1915 had, therefore, to seek for a solution to the problem of fronts locked by fire and fortification. They first sought it mainly in the use of concentrated artillery, and particularly of heavy artillery. Changes in the construction of guns had made it possible to bring into action, in slow-moving war, guns of a size greater than any except those old bombards of the far past used in the siege of cities. The big howitzer, firing a ton or so of metal, had been added by the Germans to the equipment of their field armies.

The essential way in which these guns differed from those of past centuries was that the recoil was mechanically absorbed by a system of springs or compression chambers or friction brakes which were part of the gun itself. From the first mortars on their immense wooden platforms to the field guns of Napoleon's day or of the Crimean War, the recoil due to the firing of the gun caused the whole weapon to move backward. Before it was fired, every member of the crew had to be clear of the whole area into which the gun might jump. And as soon as the gun had been fired, it had to be moved back to its original position and resighted. This told against speed and accuracy.

The guns of the past were fired by black powder, which made such a smoke that on a still day the gunners had to wait for a moment or two after firing their weapon and running it back into position before they could aim it again. The development of smokeless powders and of more powerful propellants had cut out this difficulty, and had also made it possible for gun positions to be relatively invisible to the enemy.

But the development that really speeded up artillery fire was that of the breech-lock. A gun loaded by the muzzle was difficult and slow to sponge out and to load and fire; and the gunners had to expose themselves in front of their weapon for each round. As breech-loading came in, it became possible for artillery to be worked by gunners who remained in relative safety behind shields attached to their weapons or behind earthworks. And the process was far swifter, so that a field gun could pour out several shells a minute as compared with one shell every few minutes.

With this improved artillery, many soldiers believed, in 1915, it should be possible to do what Napoleon had done in the past: blast a hole through the opponent's line and then send forward infantry (or even cavalry) through the gap and round the flanks on each side of it. Most of the history of the war of 1914-18 is the history of the failure of this idea. Guns and howitzers could be made that would, when concentrated, slowly churn up the earth and destroy the trenches in which defending infantry were hiding. One answer to this was the deep dugout, such as those made by the Germans under the Hindenburg Line. But in the main the heavy artillery of that war provided its own answer. The aim was penetration of the enemy's line; the guns could smash up earth and trenches, but in doing so they made an impassable barrier in front of themselves, a barrier of torn fields in which the drainage was destroyed, of shell-holes and ruined paths, through which it was difficult for the infantry to penetrate and quite impossible for the artillery itself to get forward. These guns were siege weapons, and this warfare was often treated as siege warfare. But in fact it differed from a normal siege because new 'walls' could be created more easily and quickly than old 'walls' could be knocked down. Behind each breach made in a defensive system, in this trench warfare, new lines of trenches could be dug and manned before the attacking force could get its guns up over the desert of mud and ruin that they had themselves created.

The guns had been improved, but the means of transporting them had not. No pneumatic tires existed large enough or strong enough even for the field guns. The larger, heavier weapons, with steel tires on their wheels, would knock any road to pieces even if moved only at the pace of the slowest cart horse. Howitzers used to be dragged forward by steam traction engines. And on the Western Front men, more numerous than any army Wellington ever commanded, spent their lives through years of warfare remaking roads that the guns destroyed with their wheels almost as much as with their shells.

Surprise dropped out of warfare. Every attack was a frontal attack, and the probable place and date for it was given away by the artillery preparation. And no attack could be concentrated on a narrow front to achieve a break-through, partly because the immense concentration of munitions required had to be brought up near the line and stored in dumps; as these dumps spread out from each railhead laterally, they could only feed the attack on a relatively wide front. The railroads were the main means of transport for supplies; motor transport was used for only a few troop movements and for the distribution of supplies between railhead and the dumps. Horse transport was still standard both, for infantry and guns. Armies were closely tied, not only to their railroads, but to the great dumps of ammunition which these fed. It was not unusual for these dumps to include about ten thousand tons of ammunition. If the army desired to move forward or backward, it would take days to lift such supplies and transport them. Very occasionally they were lifted much more rapidly, by enemy air bombardment or by accident. Nine thousand tons of shells went up at Audruicq in 1916, and ten thousand at Saigneville and ten thousand at Blangies during 1918. Before an offensive, in this form of war, it might be necessary to create a dozen dumps of this size. The amount of ammunition expended in 1916, in one month's bombardment on the Somme, was 148,000 tons. By 1918 even more incredible amounts of steel and high-explosive were being poured out. The artillery preparation at the third battle of Ypres lasted for ten days and was carried out by over three thousand guns, of which a thousand were heavy. This was an average of one gun to every six yards of front. Four and a quarter million shells were fired, costing $110,000,000. Four and three-quarters tons of shells were thrown on every linear yard of front.

And the result? The result was that at great cost of lives some square miles of swamp were gained; this swamp had been made impassable for guns or tanks by our own shells and almost impassable for troops.

The war of 1914-18 has been discussed endlessly; the offensive we have just described has been one of the battles most bitterly fought in books and newspapers, perhaps as bitterly fought as on the ground. Mr. Lloyd George bases much of his criticism of Haig on this costly and futile offensive. Now that we are in a very different sort of war, it is easier to see 1914-18 in perspective; it is easier to see that there was an element of the inevitable about these suicidal massacres in the mud. It was not any general's fault that they occurred; they were not due to the prejudices or mistakes of a staff or a caste of officers. They were due to the whole shape and nature of war as war then existed, a shape and nature imposed on war by the natural development of weapons. And behind that development of weapons were all the swift changes of the Machine Age, the changes in industrial technique and social life. The effects of these changes are described by Winston Churchill in words that I have quoted before but cannot better:

> Wealth, science, civilisation, patriotism, steam transport, and world credit enabled the whole strength of every belligerent to be continually applied to the war. The entire populations fought and laboured, women and men alike, to the utmost of their physical destructiveness. National industry was in every country converted to the production of war material. Tens of millions of soldiers, scores of thousands of cannon, hurled death across the battle lines, themselves measured in thousands of miles. Havoc on such a scale had never even been dreamed of in the past, and had never proceeded at such a speed in all human history. To carry this process to the final limit was the dearest effort of every nation, and of nearly all that was best and noblest in every nation.
>
> But at the same time that Europe had been fastened into this frightful bondage, the art of war had fallen into an almost similar helplessness. No means of procuring a swift decision presented itself to the strategy of the commanders, or existed on the battlefields of the armies. The chains which held the warring nations to their task were not destined to be severed by military genius; no sufficient

> preponderance of force was at the disposal of either side; no practical method of decisive offensive had been discovered.[1]

This helplessness of the art of war, we can see now, was due to the slowness with which armies changed away from an old conception of warfare to a new one. All the technical means for ending 'this helplessness' were present early in the war; the gasoline engine, the caterpillar tractor, the idea of an armoured vehicle capable of crossing trenches and standing machine-gun fire, the aeroplane and the light machine-gun were all available. What was not available was the idea of war as a changing art of science affected by every change in the techniques of production and transport, and inevitably out of date if these techniques were not employed to the full. The generals who were responsible for tactics and strategy, for advice to governments and demands on industry, had to take first responsibility for the failure to change when change was possible. They had a heavier responsibility: they definitely and deliberately obstructed change. But looking beyond them, and seeing their figures shrunk to the measure of reality, one sees that these generals, with rare exceptions, were the last people to be expected to welcome and develop new changes in their jobs; between the time when they first learned warfare and the time when they came to command, the job had grown so much more rapidly than they had, and had already changed so much more than they expected, that they could not be expected to be pioneers of change.

None of the general staffs had expected that artillery would possess the overwhelming importance that I have been stressing as the characteristic feature of 1914-18.

[1] Winston Churchill, *The World Crisis, 1916-18,* Part I, page 19.

The Germans were nearest to reality in their pre-war estimates, and therefore scored in their early battles by bringing to action the huge howitzers that British and French staffs thought only fit for siege work. But the Germans had calculated on a short war and had not prepared sufficient stocks of shells for trench warfare. From all the armies, therefore, in 1915 there was a clamour for more shells, and each of the nations at war found it necessary to mobilise women for the shell-filling factories. In parliaments and in newspapers so much attention was given to 'shell shortages' that public opinion came to view the production of guns and munitions as the essential key to victory in war. The bitter war weariness of later years came largely from the fact that this key failed to open any door to victory. Artillery had become the dominant weapon, but was not the decisive weapon.

The difference between these two ideas requires explanation. Artillery in Napoleon's hands had been the decisive weapon, though not the dominant one, the one most used to kill enemy soldiers. He had used it to secure decision by preparing the way for his infantry columns. It no longer secured such decisions. But artillery was the dominant weapon, in 1914-18, because in those years it killed most enemy soldiers and did most damage to their defences and was the most effective weapon for hampering movement behind the front line. Some incomplete figures exist that show the change very sharply. These are official German figures, quoted by Shirlaw and Troke in *Medicine versus Invasion:*

	Wounds caused by infantry (per cent)	Wounds caused by artillery (per cent)
1870-71	91.6	8.4
1914-15	22.3	49.29
1916-18	6.0	85.0

Clearly there are points of difficulty about these figures. Were no wounds caused by cavalry in 1870-71? Why are the figures for 1914-15 so incomplete? They add up to less than seventy-two per cent. Does it seem likely that the figures for 1914-15 can be accurate to two places of decimals, while those for the later years of that war work out at round-figure percentages? I should not like to accept such calculations if my argument depended on their accuracy. It does not. My argument is based on the main tendency they show, and on a belief that the real percentages were somewhere near these figures. In the war of 1870-71, infantry did about ten times as much killing as artillery; less than fifty years later, artillery was doing about ten times as much killing as infantry. That is the essential point. An immense change had occurred, and more than half that change had happened before 1914. Yet the relative importance of guns and rifles seemed to Sir John French and his staff in 1914 little different from the relative importance of guns and muskets in Wellington's time.

By 1915 the new ideas were spreading; shell shortages, the need for long artillery preparation, 'the artillery wins the ground, the infantry occupies it.' An inevitable consequence of these (then new) ideas was that surprise no longer mattered in attack. Sir John French, the British Commander-in-Chief, wrote on May 14, 1915, to a subordinate charged with command in an offensive:

> As the element of surprise will now be absent (owing to the long artillery preparation) it is probable that your progress will not be rapid.

Progress certainly was not rapid; and only on large-scale maps could it be discovered at all.

> In short, surprise was abandoned [writes Captain G. C. Wynne] and the long bombardment and so-called 'war of attrition' began. The consequence was that the artillery now became the chief weapon of offence, while the infantry arm, dethroned from its place as queen of the battlefield, became its kitchen-maids or 'moppers-up,' and any method of procedure was accordingly regarded as a matter of minor importance.[2]

Captain Wynne (who uses the word 'procedure' to mean what we now call 'battle drill' or basic tactics) has described, in the book quoted, the problem that Sir John French and other commanders had stumbled against. This was, in essence, the defensive power of well-placed machine-guns. I cannot here go into the wealth of detail which he uses to demonstrate the German development of defence by machine-gun strong-points from the first crude rigid forms of this defence to the flexible deep defences of 1918. But the reader who wants the essence of the tactics of 1914-18 in miniature cannot do better than refer to pages 42 to 59 of his book.

In these pages Captain Wynne shows how two basic theories of war conflicted in 1915. The question was

> whether the infantry was to have the covering fire and support of artillery and every form of mechanised aid to help its own skilfully organised forward movement, or whether the artillery and every form of mechanised weapon were to have the infantry to 'mop up' what

[2] *If Germany Attacks,* page 52.

> they intended first to conquer; whether, in a few words, fire-effect and movement should work simultaneously together, or whether fire-effect should be followed by movement. British G.H.Q. and French G.Q.G. adopted the latter, fire-effect followed by movement, while the German O.H.L. kept to the doctrine which all armies had previously followed, fire-effect combined with movement; and that distinction is still, to this day, the fundamental difference between the latest (1939) training manuals of the French Army, on the one hand, and of the German, on the other.[3]

Fire and movement together can be decisive; fire divorced from movement can kill millions, wear out armies and states, and eventually end a war by the exhaustion of one side a little before the other side exhausts itself. The decision taken in 1915, on our side, was to divorce fire from movement, killing from manoeuvre, and to hand the main business of battle over to the guns. After they had done their worst, in bombardments lasting days or weeks, the infantry would flounder forward into the resulting devastation.

But there was an alternative decision that could have been taken. A new 'procedure' was possible, new battle tactics. This alternative belongs to the next chapter. It opens the new phase of war, the phase of the present day, which begins with the word 'infiltration' and has developed to the stage described by the word *Blitzkrieg*. But before we start on a new chapter, with this phase of war as

[3] *Ibid.*, page 59.

its theme, it is necessary to complete our study of artillery as the dominant weapon in 1914-18, and the machine-gun as the decisive weapon.

I have already, as best I can, defined my use of these terms. I use 'dominant' to mean the main arm, to the creation of which during war nations turn most of their powers, on the use of which generals and staffs concentrate their hopes and energies. A 'dominant weapon,' to my mind, is that which causes most casualties to the enemy, and does most of the job of battle. But a 'decisive weapon' is more important. It achieves decision, the end of the battle, victory. It dictates changes in the shape of war. The machine-gun, not the field piece or the howitzer, governed the shape of 1914-18. It did so first by 'locking the fronts'; then in new ways it 'unlocked' them. The tank is a device for combining the fire of machine-guns (and of weapons able to root out machine-guns) with movement through machine-gun fire. Infiltration is a way of getting your own machine-guns forward through the enemy's machine-gun strong-points. As far as there was any real shape to the art of war in 1914-18, that shape was formed by Maxim's invention, together with the trench and the barbed-wire entanglement. And as far as there was any real decision in that indecisive war, the machine-gun was the main factor in producing it.

9
Tank and Plane

In this chapter we carry the story of weapons and tactics as far as the changes obvious before the main campaigns of 1942. The whole story, as we have dealt with it so far, covers three thousand years or more from the Siege of Troy to the four-year siege of Germany in 1914-18. The present chapter covers less than thirty years, not one per cent of the whole. Yet it contains so much of change, so immense a revolution in warfare, that the changes of the past seem to be dwarfed by those made obvious even in the three years 1939-42, while other and possibly even greater changes loom up ahead of us, their outlines seen vaguely through the fog of war and the thicker fog of censorship.

I summarise the main changes, and only the main changes, of the years between 1917 and 1942 as the development of deep infiltration as a basic tactical principle, and the development of new weapons that, used together, become for a period decisive—the essential feature of these weapons, the tank and the plane, being that they can move very much more rapidly than any decisive weapons hitherto possessed by armies. With these changes attack, which had been far more costly than defence, becomes cheaper in lives and material than defence.

Decisive strategic manoeuvre had for three thousand years before 1917 been tied to the pace of men marching.

Very occasionally this pace had been doubled or trebled to that of men riding fast. During 1914-18 many movements of strategic importance were made by rail. But the movements were all behind locked fronts. Not until tanks and planes were fully developed, and used together in a way suited to their capacities, was the average speed of decisive manoeuvre, capable of tactically 'unlocking' the enemy front, raised from the three miles an hour of the marching man to the ten, twenty, or thirty miles an hour of the gasoline-driven vehicle.

In an introductory chapter we singled out mobility, hitting power, and protection as probably the most important factors (with morale) in battle. Mobility in these brief thirty years changes from feet to wheels or wings. Hitting power changes less; but with the development of the bomber at one end of the scale, and of the submachine-gun at the other, the weapons of today have hundreds of times increased the range of hitting power and several times increased its concentration at close quarters. Meanwhile, protection has undergone a change more radical than either of the other two; it has changed, not merely by quantity becoming quality, but by an essential change in its nature. Protection is no longer mainly given by earthworks; it is mainly given by armour and by invisibility.

The tank was at first a weapon that *restored* mobility, but did not greatly *increase* mobility either tactically or strategically. The first tanks travelled at three or four miles an hour, and like the airplanes of 1914-18 their range was very limited. They were thought of, by those who first proposed them and brought them into being against the vigorous opposition of official military opinion, as moving machine-gun platforms sufficiently armoured to protect their crews from machine-gun fire, and sufficiently mobile to go ahead of infantry and clear a way for them. This remained their principal function, even in the views of their most devoted admirers, until at the battle of Cambrai, late in 1917, they showed that they were inherently capable of offensive movement so rapid as to leave the infantry far behind them. In other words, they showed themselves capable of a decisive operation: the breach of the enemy's position. The function that had been performed long ago by the armoured phalanx of foot-soldiers, and later by the armoured 'battle' of knights, was after 1917 possible, achievable, by the modern armoured force. This function was not in fact carried out fully by an armoured force during the next twenty years or more, until the battle of Aragon in 1938. But in 1918, French and British tanks showed even more successfully than at Cambrai that they possessed the power to achieve a break-through, and that the question of developing this break-through into decisive manoeuvre was a question of how to support the tanks, how to speed up the available support for them.

The tank itself grew up rapidly; and at first all its development was towards greater speed. All the French tanks of 1917, and half the British, carried machine-guns only as their weapons. Their tactical value was that they added to this decisive weapon, the machine-gun, the power to move. Half of the British tanks, however, carried two six-pounder guns each. They carried these particular guns because these were naval guns which the Admiralty found it possible to spare; the War Office did not find it possible to spare, or to make, any such armament for tanks. In fact, the War Office attitude to tanks was mainly confined to cancelling the orders given to construct them, whittling down the construction programmes when these were forced through by Cabinet Ministers, and staffing the Tank Corps with officers who had in some way gained a reputation for 'difficulty.' Luckily this type of officer was, under the social conditions then reigning in the British Army, often the best available for a new arm developing new tactics. And it is remarkable how soon the officers of the Tank Corps developed a clear sense of the possibilities of their arm. For this much of the credit is due to Major-General J. F. C. Fuller, whose autobiography, *Memoirs of an Unconventional Soldier,* contains a blistering description of the military conservatism which delayed or prevented correct use of tanks.

By 1918, whippet tanks were in action, capable of four or five times the speed of the first models. These tanks showed their capacity on August 8, 1918, by penetrating up to and beyond the enemy's artillery positions and divisional and corps headquarters. In other words, this weapon was now capable of piercing the whole depth of a normal defensive position; what it could not do was take with it the infantry and artillery to hold the ground won. The problem of support and occupation remained unsolved in 1918; it was first solved in 1938 during the Spanish Civil War, when airplanes as artillery support for tanks (and particularly the first dive-bombers used in action), and truck-borne infantry for occupation of ground won, supplied the two necessary ingredients to make the armoured division the decisive unit in a period of warfare.

The airplane developed during 1914-18 even more rapidly than any other weapon. The first large bomber ordered by the British Admiralty in 1914 was intended to have a speed of 72 miles per hour and to carry six 112-pound bombs. It was powered by two engines, each of which developed 255 horsepower. This was considered a 'giant' in those days; my own first flight was taken in a Flying Corps reconnaissance machine of 70 horsepower without armament and only capable of lifting a bomb if the passenger seat was empty. Normal armament on the 90 horsepower machines used by the first squadron to which I was posted in France, in 1916, was a single machine-gun which could only fire towards the rear. These observation planes mainly worked for the massed artillery of those days, observing shell bursts and correcting range. Air bombardment on the battlefield or close behind it was of practically no importance; occasional longer raids on railways, road junctions, or dumps were only of importance because they slowly forced on the armies the need to move at night or during bad flying conditions.

By the end of that war the average speed of fighter planes had nearly doubled, though heavy bombers were still fantastically slow. In 1918, a four-engined bomber, the Handley-Page V 1500, was available to bomb Berlin. Its weight loaded was thirty thousand pounds as compared with eight thousand pounds for the 1914 'giant' mentioned; it carried a number of machine-guns for its own protection; it could have carried one thousand pounds of bombs to Berlin. Equivalent development had taken place in fighters; and special types of machines had been designed to intervene directly on the battlefield either by bombing or by ground strafing. But the airplane during that war, though its development was rapid, was only in its infancy. At no time did any air force have one-tenth the hitting power of the artillery of its army.

Twenty years later, during the war in Spain, air power had become adult, and General Franco's bombers normally dropped as many thousand tons of bombs on a battlefield as his artillery did of shells. The figures for the operations which, put together, constitute General Franco's counter-offensive on the Ebro in the autumn of 1938 are nine thousand tons of artillery projectiles and over eight thousand tons of bombs. It is probable that subsequent German campaigns in Poland and France would also show a rough equality between these two forms of bombardment. By 1938, therefore, air power had become capable of taking over a large share of the functions of artillery. In particular it could take over the function of supporting tanks and motorised infantry. As a flying artillery, planes could do what guns used to do in Napoleon's hands: blast open a breach in the enemy's position for decisive manoeuvre. From 1938 it was clear that the dive-bomber was the best type of plane for this decisive function.

Meanwhile, the third factor necessary for the modern armoured unit was developing through the normal civilian development of road transport. A truck in 1916 was a clumsy machine put together by hand and not designed for large-scale manufacture. By 1936, thanks to Mr. Ford and those who imitated or improved on him, trucks could be turned out of vast factories, in which they flowed together on assembly lines, by the hundred thousand. Whole divisions or army corps could move at the same speed as the tanks, only jumping down from the vehicles to go into action.

The speed of tactical manoeuvre thus in a few years leapt from three miles per hour or less to a possible thirty miles per hour or more. Normal speeds were ten to twelve miles per hour. But the speed of strategic manoeuvre did not increase to the same extent. For various reasons—difficulties of road congestion, need to refuel vehicles, and need to shelter tanks at night are among these reasons—the armies on wheels and tracks that the Germans poured across Europe between 1939 and the end of 1941 did not often move in decisive force at a speed greater than forty-five to sixty miles per day. Perhaps they did not need to move faster; the armies opposing them could be pierced, severed into fragments, and shattered by strategic moves that went at this pace. These armies all depended, in defence, ultimately on their power to move infantry on the roads. Like the Germans, these armies possessed trucks; like the Germans again, they had also ordinary infantry divisions, without much transport, that moved by marching. The essential fact was that the Germans were on the offensive; these armies on the defensive. For strategic offensive manoeuvre against some part of the enemy's position, and towards key points behind that position, the Germans could use their fast-moving troops; for the shifting of troops not attacked, and reserves, towards the point of battle, the opponents of the Germans had to move troops by foot as well as by truck. They had not recognised the dominance, in that period of warfare, of the armoured and motorised 'combat team.' Because of this their armies had not so organised their forces and their transport to make possible a counter to German blows, a counter-blow struck with great tactical rapidity and with a strategic rapidity rather higher than that possible for forces marching on foot. Men have marched, under special conditions, sixty miles within twenty-four hours. But they cannot often do so; and their value as fighting units is decreased by exhaustion and lack of sleep. Normally for marching armies strategic manoeuvre at the rate of sixteen miles a day is fairly good going. The Germans were going over twice this pace, and therefore were able to divide and get behind their antagonists, surrounding and trapping portions of their armies.

This is the story of the Polish campaign, the fall of France, the campaigns in Greece and Libya during 1941, and the opening stages of the Russian campaign in the autumn of that year. This is the *Blitzkrieg*. It is a system of weapons and tactics capable of piercing an enemy's position (if defended by troops trained mainly according to the methods of 1914-18 or the British and French methods of 1939), and destroying the enemy army by encircling some part of it; by the speed and vigour of the break-through, this system of tactics tears out a flank, or several flanks, in the enemy's continuous line and then attacks the severed portions of that line from the flank or rear.

The development of new weapons, which, through their speed of tactical and strategic manoeuvre, become of decisive importance, is one half of the *Blitzkrieg;* the other half is the development of new tactics, the tactics of infiltration raised to a new level and a new speed.

The first idea of modern infiltration we can trace occurred in the mind of a French infantry captain, André Laffargue, whose company was attacking (with of course many other French troops on each side of it) towards Vimy Ridge on the ninth of May, 1915. In spite of heavy losses his company broke through the German trenches and captured a ruined village beyond them. A long bare slope ahead of them, rising to the crest of Vimy Ridge, seemed empty of the enemy. Then two German machine-guns opened up, from a 'nest' which covered this slope. They were the only opposition, but in that area they held up the whole attack. For four hours Laffargue's company and another French company lay waiting for the German machine-guns to be cleared up. Then German reinforcements arrived; next day a fresh French battalion tried to advance and was stopped short mainly by the same two German machine-guns, but partly by the German reinforcements.

Captain Laffargue was intelligent; he was also exasperated. He had tried to get his own artillery, during those four hours, to drop shells on the German 'nest.' And he had realised that this artillery, at least a couple of miles behind him, could not find the target. In the pamphlet he wrote on new methods of attack he asked for heavy trench mortars right up with the front line of the attacking infantry; and he also asked for a new organisation, a new basic tactic, for part of that infantry.

Infantry in the old days of the musket had always moved forward in line; it was still moving forward in line. (I know places where it still does.) During the development of skirmishers in the Napoleonic period, the front line had become a little less regular and more widely spaced; later, all infantry became skirmishers, and became still more widely spaced. But it was still a line, and the fire from this line was mainly directed straight ahead or nearly straight ahead. Laffargue suggested that in front of the normal line of infantry two special groups of men should go from each platoon. They should be heavily armed with light automatics. And he used the word 'infiltration' to describe the way in which these small special groups should proceed.

The normal way was, then, as follows: by the time the first wave of infantry in line had reached part of the enemy trenches, much of this attacking line had normally been destroyed by fire, and many parts of the enemy trenches could not be directly assaulted from the front; the first attackers would, therefore, spread out sideways along the trenches to roll up the remaining German defenders in those trenches. This was slow and costly; the enemy knew the shape and exact position of his own trenches; his artillery, machine-guns, and defending infantry, emerging from dugouts, had great advantages over the attackers slowly bombing their way along the trench. Laffargue proposed that the two special groups ahead of each platoon attacking should press forward farther into the enemy position, through any gap they found, through communication trenches or dips in the ground or any available cover, until they were in a position to take the German machine-gun nests from the flank or from the rear. They would move forward; they would fire, not forward, but to the side, or even to some extent behind them. The German machine-guns were protected by steel plates and concrete or sandbag cover from frontal fire; they were often at this stage in the war unprotected from the rear. And they were hidden from in front, but far more visible from the rear.

The new combination of movement and fire proposed by this French officer was directed towards countering the decisive defensive weapon, the machine-gun well posted. Unluckily for us his ideas had no effect on the French Army and his pamphlet was not even translated into English. But a copy was captured by the Germans and it was found by them to be

> a concise expression of a doctrine which exactly corresponded to the course they themselves had been trying to follow by cumbersome and slow degrees. The pamphlet was at once translated into German and issued as an official German training manual, eventually becoming the basis of General Ludendorff's textbook for 'the attack in position warfare.' It was with an elaboration of Captain Laffargue's doctrine of infiltration that the Germans so effectively broke through the British position in March, 1918, and the Chemin des Dames position in the following May; and his ideas have remained the foundation of the German training manual for attack to this day.[1]

The development given to this doctrine was similar to the development of the idea of skirmishing more than a hundred years earlier. At first, in accordance with the normal process of grafting new ideas onto old ones, the infantry groups 'filtering' forward were small in proportion to the main body of the infantry attacking in line behind them. Like the skirmishers of the Napoleonic armies,

[1] Captain G. C. Wynne, *If Germany Attacks,* page 58.

they were only one-tenth or so of the troops available. Later, they became a more considerable proportion, until in the great campaigns of 1918 all German front-line troops were infiltrating, and only the reserves coming behind them were expected to attempt frontal assaults in some sort of line, to mop up centres of resistance.

For these new tactics new weapons developed. The type of machine-gun suitable for the old tactics was too heavy for the new. It was a solid piece of machinery that needed two or three men to carry it, had a water jacket to cool the barrel during continuous fire, and was used during a normal attack from positions well behind the front-line troops, or at a distance to the flank, to give them covering fire over their heads or across their front. The new tactics needed a light air-cooled weapon that could be carried by one man, to be the spearhead of the group filtering forward. And so in the middle of the war of 1914-18 we got the development of the machine-rifle or the light machine-gun such as the French Chauchat or the German Bergmann.

An immense change in training was also necessary; that change has been spread over so long a period in the British Army that its full effects are only today becoming visible. The basis of the new training is a new form of drill. The old forms of recruits' or barrack-square drill had been retained by military conservatism, in all armies, from the days when troops armed with muskets had to be trained to repel cavalry by volleys simultaneously fired, to move in close order shoulder to shoulder without breaking rank, and to maintain under all circumstances a straight alignment 'dressed by the right.' This drill became very bad training for troops whose tactics were infiltration. They no longer learned on the barrack-square anything parallel or comparable to their movements during battle. Worse than that, they were conditioned to the opposite of what they should do in battle; they were made to feel normal when doing the things that would be fatal to tactical success and to their lives. They were drilled to maintain the straight line for all too long after their only hopes of success depended on their advancing in irregular small columns or arrowhead formations moving from one patch of cover to another. It was, therefore, not surprising that new recruits, who had received little drill, often proved themselves more capable of developing these tactics than other units to whom the old tactics had become automatic through drill. This became particularly clear after 1918 when the new Red armies of the Soviet Union developed infiltration to its highest possible level, that of guerrilla or partisan fighting.

The idea of infiltration spread from minor tactics to grand tactics and to strategy. Ludendorff was not able to make this change; his great attacks of 1918 were tactical successes largely because they were carried out by the methods of infiltration; but they were not strategic successes because he never achieved such a break-through at such a speed that his forces could penetrate to the rear of the opposing armies, separate them and roll up the separated portions. It was not until the latter half of the Spanish Civil War that infiltration on this scale was worked out; and by that time the essential weapon permitting this application of the basic idea had been almost fully developed. This weapon, the modern tank, was then combined with swiftly concentrated aerial artillery and swiftly moved truck-borne infantry to produce a new type of force, capable of the strategic infiltration that is the essence and secret of the shape of the war up to the end of 1941.

Infiltration in attack at first meant the movement forward of very small bodies of infantry whose duty it was to work their way through the enemy positions and gain objectives from which they could outflank those positions or take them from the rear. During this period it was still possible, and may have been convenient, to set limited objectives for each stage in the attack. Each group attacking should only go so far forward; if they went farther forward they would get out of touch with those following them. But when this form of attack changed and became strategic infiltration, when it was carried out by vehicles rather than by troops moving on foot, the idea of limited objectives became obsolete. In the autumn of 1941 I was following large-scale British Army manoeuvres, towards the end of which a 'German' invading force was being thrown back; unfortunately, the successful commander set limited objectives for the advance of his troops, and held the more rapidly advancing units back until other units right and left of them were able to get up roughly in line with them. The result was that the more advanced of his units were unable to pierce the enemy formations; indeed, the enemy organised his withdrawal so well that within a few hours almost all his troops were thirty miles away from our 'advancing units,' most of which were not advancing at all, but were waiting for orders permitting them to advance. Strategic infiltration makes necessary the unlimited objective; the foremost attacking troops have to get as far forward, as far round the flank and rear of the enemy's forces, as they possibly can. They must not check to secure their own flanks; their speed of movement, the disturbance they cause by crashing up through the enemy's supply lines and command centres, will serve them instead of flank protection; or planes over their heads and other troops of their own army coming up through the gap they have made will protect the edges of the breach. The whole idea, therefore, of an attack by stages from one green line to the next yellow line becomes out of date in this new shape of war.

So does the idea of a wide front for the attack. If you are going through the enemy's wall in linear formation, each man shoulder to shoulder or a few yards apart, it is necessary to blow a wide hole in this wall. If your aim is to creep and wriggle behind that wall, you need only a mouse-hole to start with. And in any defensive position there is always a mouse-hole; no such defensive position can be of equal strength all along hundreds of miles of countryside.

During the Civil War in Spain the German Army carried out careful experiments on the question of the minimum width of attack necessary in order to breach defended lines of trenches. They found that in close country it was practically possible to start with a frontage of attack only about a thousand yards wide, but to be sure of results the necessary frontage was about two thousand yards. This became their standard frontage for the *Blitz* attack; and normally they attacked on two or three such frontages with gaps of about two miles between them. This was their pattern at Sedan in May, 1940, and also apparently in Libya in May, 1942.

The best analysis of this pattern is that given in *Blitzkrieg* by F. O. Miksche, a Czechoslovak officer who was a major on the general staff of the Spanish Republican Army. His book shows that the same basic tactical ideas govern the handling in battle of a section or an army corps; the German pattern of combined fire and movement gives to infiltration in the attack so brusque and rapid a character that when it is carried out on a large scale, it becomes, not a normal break-through (which can perhaps be checked and confined by reserves and the formation of new positions), but an 'irruption,' a break-through that is also the breaking-up and severing of the enemy. And he points out that the repeated success of this operation, in Poland and France, Greece and Libya, depended largely on extreme concentration of force against the narrow sectors chosen for attack. This extreme concentration was made possible by the gasoline engine. Motorisation gives the *Blitz* attack the power to penetrate almost any linear defences, because it gives the power to concentrate the force of five divisions on a mile front.

But another form of defence, a non-linear form, is possible. That form Miksche, in the book mentioned, describes in principle and in theory. It is the form known as 'web defence,' of which the basis is the holding, not of consecutive lines, but of islands of resistance capable of all-round defence, capable of continued fighting for long periods after they have been surrounded.

After Miksche's book had been written, and while it was being translated, the Nazi attack on the Soviet Union began. It began with an enormous double *Blitzkrieg,* in which the Germans drove two 'wedges' through and round the main Soviet armies on the Polish border, and joined these wedges to form what they call a *Kessel,* or basin (jacket, bulge, or cauldron), in which the Russian advanced forces were trapped. This battle of Bialystok was from the German point of view a most successful operation and according to their own figures was as large as the whole of the battle of Flanders (that is, all the fighting of May, 1940, up to and including the evacuation from Dunkirk). But one aspect of it must have made the German commanders somewhat worried about the future. Russian infantry isolated in the old fortress of Brest-Litovsk continued to resist even when isolated, and according to a German account (quoted by the United States *Infantry Journal* for April, 1942) it was necessary for the Germans to leave behind a whole infantry division to contain in this citadel 'several thousand Russian troops.' The larger Russian forces, cut off round Bialystok when the two German wedges met behind them, also continued to resist. Though surrounded, they did not surrender. And it is clear that weeks after the battle began, and even weeks after German official announcements had claimed that it was successfully ended, Russian 'islands of resistance' remained in the more difficult and marshy parts of the area. During the next three months, in fact, some of the Russian units forming these islands of resistance seem to have been fighting their way towards the Soviet lines; others were splitting up into guerrilla detachments to harry the German communications.

Although the defensive doctrine of the Red Army had not stated, or had not made clear, the idea of 'web defence,' their troops began to put this idea into action as soon as the fighting started. Part of the reason for this must have been the experiences of the Russian Civil War, in which the rapidly moving fronts and partisan and guerrilla fighting crystallised around positions defended in isolation, and particularly around towns, villages, and other road centres. Part of the reason for this development must also have been the study made in Soviet officers' schools of the development of German defensive tactics from 1915 to 1918. This German system of defence by strong-point is the main subject of Captain Wynne's book, *If Germany Attacks,* already quoted. The staffs of the Red Army must also have realised the development of defensive systems during the Spanish Civil War. This development recapitulated the development of 1914-18, and then went beyond it to a much greater depth of defence and much more reliance on the fortified strong-point.

It is sometimes forgotten now how far even the British Army's defensive system in 1918 had gone in this direction. The official *Military History of the War for 1918* compiled by Sir James E. Edmonds, states on page 257 that 'there were continuous lines of trenches in the Forward Zone, but the garrisons as a rule were disposed not in lines but in posts, strong-points, etc., for all-round defence.' The reason why this system failed in March, 1918, may be gathered from the following quotation from the same page of our official history:

> There was a general objection among the fighting officers to the distribution of the troops in small packets, the 'blob' system of defence, as it had been called, in derision, before the War, for it was not a new theory. Some even went so far as to call the policy 'suicidal'; for without strong reserves to counter-attack the enemy if he penetrated the intervals, the surrender or annihilation of the posts must be only a matter of time. The majority of experienced fighters, in view of the inadequate number of men available and lack of strong counter-attacking forces, would have preferred a definite line of resistance in each zone, with posts, machine-gun nests, and switches, arranged in depth behind it to limit any enemy entry into the line.
>
> The British soldier has times without number defended isolated posts to the death; and he did so on the 21st March, 1918, and was to do so repeatedly during the next week. But he prefers to fight in line. An old N.C.O. of 1914 summed up the new system in discussion with an officer: 'It don't suit us. The British Army fights in line and won't do any good in these bird cages.'. . .
>
> There were too many inexperienced young officers and too many untrained young soldiers to ensure a reliable garrison for every post, even without the special trial to which the fog subjected them. The platoon

> commanders were unable to exercise control over more than the posts in which they had selected to be, the section posts were unaware whether those on the flank were holding out or had been captured, with the result that there was a lack of confidence on the part of small and, on account of the weather conditions, isolated garrisons. To British troops whose instinct is to fight it out where they stand, there came no thought of 'elastic yielding,' and considerable doubt existed as to whether the garrisons, when the enemy was already in rear of them, should hold on to the last regardless of what was happening on the right or left. Some even of the best of the new officers did not realise that they must use discretion as being 'the man on the spot,' and that even orders to hold on may in extreme circumstances be disregarded. No warning seems to have been given any brigade or battalion commanders, and therefore none to the lower ranks, that in certain circumstances there might be an ordered retreat; divisional routes had been reconnoitred for this, but information of such a nature was certainly withheld from regimental officers.

It is clear from this quotation that the training of these British troops had not conditioned them to the new way of fighting. They had been drilled and exercised only to fight in line, whether attacking or defending. They had not realised that the German system of defence by strong-points, so devastatingly effective against British attack in the previous years, implied a retraining of the army in which men were not only taught new tactics, but also taught the reasons for them; or that it implied the utmost initiative by junior commanders and their readiness to move in any direction required by the course of the battle. The official history refers to the 'instinct' of British soldiers to fight where they stood. It is very difficult indeed to consider this a scientific use of the term 'instinct.' It is probable that the author means that the man had been conditioned to certain actions and attitudes of mind, and it is tragic to reflect that the same process of conditioning men, to what amounts in modern battle to stupid passivity, still continues in many parts of the British Army and even in the Home Guard.

General Ludendorff had realised the new conditions of defence by the winter of 1916 and in his *War Memories* writes of

> a more active defence . . . it was of course intended that the position should remain in our hands at the end of the battle, but the infantryman need no longer say to himself, 'Here I must stand or fall,' but had, on the contrary, the right, within certain limits, to retire in any direction before strong enemy fire.

Here, then, we have the remarkable fact that General Ludendorff, explaining the basic idea of successful German defence, and the British official history, explaining the failure of a British adaptation of this system of defence, both refer strongly and clearly to the need for retreat to be considered, when necessary, as a normal part of tactics. And no unprejudiced observer, looking at the history of British arms during that part of the present war occurring before this book was finished, would think it probable that the training of our army in the summer of 1942 should normally consist of eighty per cent training in attack, ten per cent training in the holding of positions, a small per cent of orderly withdrawal covered by a rearguard, and only in some units and in a tiny proportion, the teaching of why and when to retire, and why and when to hold on to isolated or surrounded positions. In most units the idea of withdrawal is treated as something shameful and, the idea of being cut off as something desperately dangerous. Yet the Russian defence of 1941 was necessarily based on both these ideas, and as the Russians grew accustomed to the conditions of modern fighting and developed the theory and practice of a defensive system approximating to 'web defence,' it became increasingly clear that each *Blitz* offensive by the Germans was less of an actual victory and more of a stalemate.

Then the Germans had to turn to the defensive in the Russian winter. And it soon became clear that their defensive system was based entirely on the idea of strong centres of resistance covering the railway lines and other transport facilities and capable of standing siege. One of these centres of resistance at Rhez, and another at Starya Russya, seem to have been partially or completely cut off from supplies (except by air) for most of the winter of 1941-42.

The Germans, boasting of their success after the winter was over, described these besieged centres as 'hedgehogs.' The word has a curious history, as a military term, for a defended locality. When working with F. O. Miksche on the book *Blitzkrieg* already mentioned, I published in May, 1941, a popular summary of the idea of web defence in an illustrated weekly, in which I described islands of resistance organised for all-round defence as 'bristling with arms as a hedgehog bristles with spikes.' And I wrote of the men manning certain linear posts towards the rear of a defensive system as being able, when necessary, to 'roll themselves up into new hedgehog islands.' This article was reprinted in part in a German illustrated weekly. (The general line of the German comment was: what fools these English are—look, they are only just finding out these things which we knew long ago.) Apparently the Germans liked the simile of the hedgehog, and applied it to their own islands of resistance in Russia. Some months later, General Rommel began the battle of May-June, 1942, in Libya; and one of the first dispatches to reach the British press describing the defensive tactics of British and Free French troops in this battle referred to our positions as 'hedgehogs' round which the German units flooded before being forced back.

One of the essential features in any modern system of defence, and particularly in web defence, is the use of an immense number of land mines. It is clear from descriptions of the Russian campaign that both sides use them in quantities never before employed. And it is also clear that the British defences in Libya, like General Rommel's defences south of the Bay of Sirte in an earlier phase of the campaign, now consist largely of vast minefields. In fact, the early part of Rommel's attack in May, 1942, consisted first of his opening two breaches through our minefields, then of his armoured forces forming a *Kessel* or cauldron around and behind the ten miles of minefield between the two gaps, then punching out from the rear the troops holding these ten miles, and thus widening his gap. When the main bulk of his armoured forces had flooded round the southern flank or through the original narrow gaps, and were turning back to take our defending troops between them from the rear, we got the usual optimistic Cairo stories that Rommel's armoured forces were retreating. It seems almost incredible, after so many examples have been given to the world of the normal German tactics of the *aufrollen* (the rolling-out that follows the thrust), that even the Cairo spokesman should not recognise at this late date the pattern of a *Blitz* offensive. But strange things happen in the Middle East; strangely enough, for example, the illustrated weekly in which alone the hedgehog system of defence and the large-scale minefield had been advocated—I can trace no similar advocacy in any other British periodicals—was partially banned from the Middle East by government order not long ago. This ban was not imposed in time to prevent the idea of web defence soaking into troops in Africa; but the official dislike of critical thinking, of which this ban is a tiny example, must be partly responsible for the fact that our forces in Libya, in May and June, 1942, were only partially organised for modern defence and were deployed mainly in a linear defence without depth.

It takes thorough retraining, with careful explanation, to make troops fight in a new way. Our failure in March, 1918, was due, as I have pointed out, to lack of this retraining; to quote another example from the *Official History of the War* (1918 volume, page 401):

> The enemy method of firing machine-guns in enfilade rather than straight to the front led the partially trained troops to imagine that they were being fired on from behind or outflanked, and they often retired for this reason alone.

Partially trained troops to whom the new tactics have not been properly explained will always be made uneasy, if not useless, by enemy infiltration. How much of our failure in June, 1942, in Libya was due to this factor cannot yet be judged at the time of writing. But clearly the lack of modern tactical theory and of retraining on that theory was largely responsible for earlier disasters, for Singapore and Burma, for example.

The pattern of *Blitz* warfare includes other elements that will be noted in the next chapter, in which I attempt to analyse the probable future tendencies in warfare. They need to be noted here, briefly, to complete our outline of the changes in weapons and tactics up to the full development of the *Blitzkrieg*. The first, and to the popular mind the most striking, is the development of air-borne troops—parachutists and troops landed from carrier planes and gliders. Such troops played a minor part, but one of importance, in the battle of Flanders. They have only once, at this writing, played a decisive rôle in battle: they took Crete. They will have more importance in the future.

The second element is the development of armed civilians, as Home Guards or guerrillas, and the whole development of guerrilla warfare to a scale of world importance. The importance of this aspect of modern tactics is considerable; I argue in the next chapter that it will become the decisive factor in war.

Then a third element in the pattern of Blitz warfare: the shaping of protective weapons, anti-tank and anti-aircraft, with which to answer and check the new dominant tank-plane combination. These protective weapons have a history of their own; they begin as things separated, organisationally and tactically, from the normal weapons of infantry. They end as infantry weapons, closely and organically connected with the men who, without them, can be cancelled from the battlefield. Among these weapons some show a significant tendency towards a multiplication of functions. Thus, the German 88-millimetre gun is first an anti-aircraft weapon, then becomes in addition a field gun, and then becomes the most powerful antitank gun in normal use. It changes in this way from a single-purpose weapon to a triple-purpose weapon during a year of fighting in Spain. And the whole idea or principle of several purposes or functions in a weapon is so alien to our military conservatism that this gun is a 'surprise' in Libya in 1942, five years after it had first been used in these three ways.

Infantry, in this period of the *Blitzkrieg,* is an arm that fights tanks and planes as well as men. It can do so only if it is given new weapons: explosives, anti-tank mines and grenades, anti-aircraft and anti-tank guns. It is at the same time given field guns, directly under the control of the infantry or regimental commanders, because, owing to the rapidity of movement of modern battle, there is no longer time for separate arms in separate organisations to function together. In this way an infantry brigade or regiment becomes a unit of all arms, and even smaller units become self-contained 'little armies on their own.' This process develops in the direction indicated by the words 'combat team': any part of a fighting force at any time tends to become a team of several arms closely integrated together.

On the same principle air, sea, and land forces are integrated by the Germans in what they call their *Wehrmacht,* a single fighting force under a single command and a single staff. Each of the smaller units that make up this fighting force, whether they contain ships and planes, or ships and troops, or all three together, is given a single commander; and the three arms are further linked (as within the ground forces each part of the combat team is linked to the others) by radio. This is used in action without the slow and painful business of coding and decoding still imposed on our forces by an out-of-date idea of security; the Germans sending messages in plain language protect their security by speed of action rather than by hampering attempts at secrecy.

These, then, are some of the lesser developments of the *Blitzkrieg* pattern of warfare, the pattern that has dominated the present war until 1942. But in that pattern we should not allow these smaller threads to obscure the main design. The main thing in the design of modern war, from the Aragon battle of 1938 to the Libyan fighting of 1942, is a revival of the armoured phalanx, of the concentrated column hitting hard on a narrow front, armour on tracks and wheels playing the same rôle as the armoured foot-soldier of Alexander or of Caesar or the armoured chivalry of William the Conqueror. This armoured phalanx was handled in a new way. Because it provided a dangerous target when massed closely together, a target for enemy bombers or long-range artillery, it can only be massed when needed for decisive action, for the break-through. Over and over again I have heard the complaint, from those fighting in Libya and the Western desert, that our tanks were scattered when General Rommel's tanks were concentrated. Most of those who complained stated the lesson of these campaigns to be the concentration of armour. Yet, on June 13, 1942, the decisive action in the last of these campaigns to take place while this book was being written, our own concentrated armour was destroyed by enemy gunfire. And occasionally we have heard of General Rommel's tanks being so scattered about the desert that our own forces could not find them and bring them to action. It is clear that German tank tactics include alternating concentration and dispersion.

They concentrate for the *schwerpunkt,* the rolling thrust that zigzags through an enemy dispersed in defensive positions; having achieved their break-through, they fan out in the *aufrollen* to find the next weak point, to take defensive positions from the rear and to exploit their penetration to the full. Faced by new resistance they concentrate again to by-pass it or break through it, and then fan out again. And this alternating concentration and dispersion is the essential tactical pattern, not merely of the *Panzer* divisions, but of all German combat teams however formed.

This pattern of tactics has the same essential shape on the map as the movement of Napoleon's army corps and divisions during a campaign. These forces marched separately, but struck together. Between battles they spread out, not merely to have room in which to live and move (and live off the country), but in order to overlap and threaten from different angles the enemy's positions. The tactics of the armoured phalanx, and of modern combinations of infantry and other arms, are not tactics derived simply from the weapons that modern industry produces or from some theory or skill of the Germans. They are tactics embodying in a modern shape all the proved expedients of the masters of warfare from Alexander's day to Napoleon. Their aim is decision by envelopment—by pressing and jamming the enemy closely together, as the legions were pressed at Cannae or the Austrians at Leuthen—and envelopment is sought by a swift irruption that divides the enemy's army. They are tactics that can be justified by reference to Epaminondas or to Clausewitz. It is surely time they were recognised as valid by those who control our armies; and recognised also by them and our people as necessary methods that must be learned before we can go beyond them.

10
Change Goes On

The essence of the thing I have been trying to do in this book is not statement of a pattern of war; it is statement of a pattern of change in war. I have not been trying to establish the thesis that this, that, or the other is the essential feature of modern tactics; I have been trying to establish that modern tactics are changing, as modern weapons are changing, more rapidly than ever before; but that the lines on which they are changing parallel the lines of past change and should be to some extent predictable. And it is only if we can predict, foresee, the lines along which war is changing that we shall be able to establish a 'doctrine' of warfare, an integrated system of choice and design of weapons and retraining for new tactics, which will not merely rival the methods of our enemies, but will go beyond them, and be superior to them.

The first tendency in any armoured period, as we have already pointed out, is towards the creation of a force whose essential shape is that of the phalanx—a 'heavy hammer' of armour. Tanks were not used in this way when they were first invented. In 1917 or 1918, tanks went into the attack spaced out in 'waves' or lines, each machine fifty or a hundred yards away from its neighbour to right or left of it and each wave followed at some distance by another wave. And this remained the typical method of tank attack in most manoeuvres between the two great wars and in the early stages of the Spanish Civil War. In the middle of that war, after some tentative experiments near Balboa, the Germans first tried massing one hundred and fifty tanks on a narrow front to achieve a break-through in Aragon. A little later, army manoeuvres in Germany showed that the idea of a phalanx of tanks had been adopted as the Nazi solution for the stalemate of trench warfare. Later still, in the Polish Corridor and at Sedan and in the Monastir Gap and on the plains of the Ukraine, the Germans showed us in detail the methods of the *Blitz* attack of which the spearhead is the phalanx of tanks. It normally included, before 1942, the massing of all medium and heavy tanks of a division—say two hundred machines—in a combat echelon advancing on a front five hundred to seven hundred yards wide. This frontage would be filled by perhaps twenty tanks, each about thirty yards away from its neighbours on either side, and each of these twenty machines leading a file or column containing nine others, spaced at intervals perhaps a little greater. This combat echelon, therefore, when at rest would cover a square of ground each side of which would be about one-third of a mile. Its advance would be covered by lighter units and by engineers specially trained to deal with anti-tank obstacles; behind it would come truck-borne infantry and mobile guns to mop up and to widen the breach made in the enemy's defences. It was a combination that was irresistible—until Moscow and Leningrad resisted it.

At some point in the autumn of 1941, it became apparent that the period of the armoured force as a heavy hammer was probably ending, on the Russian front. It could still continue to be used in this way by Rommel in Africa against a defence that neglected depth; it could only be used once or twice more in this way, effectively, against the Russian defence, which was all depth, which consisted of hundreds of miles of guerrillas, combat troops, counter-attack troops, fortified towns, and the reserves, from front to rear. And at the same time there appeared an obvious contradiction between the type of force the Germans were using and the functions for which that force was intended. A heavy hammer does not infiltrate. We have described the team, or combination of tanks, planes, and truck-borne infantry, as the necessary combination for long-range strategic infiltration; but this grouping of tanks into a phalanx—ideal for penetrating a linear defence—was obviously unsuitable for continued infiltration over immense areas of a web defence. The phalanx was intended for a single sharp decisive hammer blow lasting only a few hours; then the tanks should be dispersed in the *aufrollen;* to keep these tanks together in a mass when enemy bombers might find them, or enemy artillery catch them while a concentrated target, was to take enormous risks. Therefore, by the time the campaigns of 1942 opened, tanks were no longer used in this way on the Russian front, or were used in this way extremely rarely.[1] And the *Panzer* division of 1942 had fewer tanks in it, and more guns, infantry, planes, and pioneers.

Turn back to my second chapter and glance again at the brief summary of how fighting changed from Epaminondas to Alexander. The heavy Macedonian phalanx had to be split up into more manoeuvrable brigades and integrated with other arms, with light troops and troops using projectile weapons and all the rest. A process strikingly similar to this has been going on in Russia. And the Russians are ahead in the development of this process. It

1 'A fortnight ago a surprise announcement was made to foreign journalists by the militarists of the Wilhelmstrasse: The *Panzer* spearhead is no more, they said in effect.' *London Evening Standard,* July 24, 1942.

is clear that they began their war in June, 1941, with a much less definite idea than the Germans about the use of the armoured phalanx, but a much more definite idea than the Germans about the need for a combination of all arms and all methods of fighting, a combination in which infantry recovers its premier place on the battlefield. And as the German massed tanks lost their impetus and were forced to divide into smaller packets in order to carry out deeper infiltration, or to attack on wider fronts without hope of decisive irruption, the Russians gained (at a heavy cost) the necessary practical experience which gave them the power to group around their tank brigades, and group above them, the other arms and forces with which these brigades became integrated.

The tank still remains the dominant weapon, just as, long after Alexander, the armoured foot-soldier of the Roman legion remained dominant in battle. But it can only achieve its ends when part of a combat team of mixed arms. The typical German armoured division of 1940 was already becoming such a combat team; it possessed its own aircraft and artillery, its own regiment or regiments of mobile infantry, its own engineer or pioneer units for the construction or destruction of anti-tank defences. But what the Russians seem to have done goes beyond this: their tank brigades and divisions are flexibly united with the infantry, and any unit consisting mainly of infantry may have as a constituent part of it either tanks or planes or both, if these are needed for its function. Commanders of such combat teams are no longer purely infantry commanders or tank commanders; they are in the old sense of the words 'general officers,' that is to say, officers taking a general command of all the arms and troops engaged in an action. No other sort of general is possible today.

Tanks were tragically mishandled during the period 1917 to 1938, when they were tied closely to infantry advancing in line on foot. Then for a period, the period of the classical *Blitzkrieg,* they were released to prove their power to achieve the break-through against linear defence. But then they came up against defences, in Russia, that they could not break through; these defences could be said to extend throughout the depth of the whole country. No 'irruption' could get beyond them; there was no beyond. In order to muscle and wrestle farther and farther into this web—like a man wading through an underbrush of flypapers—each armoured force had to become a complete 'army on its own'; and each of these combat teams had to split down into smaller teams for mopping up here, for further penetration there, for seeking a weak point in this or that direction. The forces infiltrating were being themselves filtered. And the defensive filter was designed with a special aim in view: to hold back the enemy infantry and separate them from the armoured forces. This, indeed, is the main aim of web defence—to cut the armoured spearhead off from the body of the spear that follows it. And because this is the aim, forces attacking against web defence have to carry to the farthest limits possible the process we have been describing, the integration of infantry and armour. This integration is tactically carried to its limit when tanks attacking form a hollow square within which truck-borne infantry move forward.

The development of warfare in the past thirty years has greatly altered the traditional relation of infantry to other arms. In 1915 and 1916, infantry ceased to be 'the queen of the battlefield' and the theory was developed that 'artillery conquers the ground and the infantry occupies it.' Then, in 1938-39, the new theory and practice was developed by which the tanks conquer the ground and the infantry occupies it. But already this is changing. Though there are more tanks and planes than ever, the fighting value of infantry in its new form, as main constituent and basis for combat teams of all arms, is steadily increasing. I believe it will increase further, that infantry will be again the decisive arm. But it will only be so by taking to itself and making part of itself the dominant arms—tanks, planes, and artillery—and by moving before action and to some extent during action at the speed possible to vehicles. I do not believe that we are going back from the *Blitzkrieg* to Verdun; manoeuvre by vehicle will continue to be the decisive form of manoeuvre. But in manoeuvre by vehicle the emphasis will change from manoeuvre by tanks backed by infantry towards manoeuvre by mechanised infantry protected by tanks. The change may not seem a great one. But in every practical aspect of training for attack and defence, and of planning and carrying out these operations, this change of emphasis will make the difference between a real victory and a Pyrrhic one. For a period, even against web defence, massed tanks may still win their Pyrrhic victories, as the Macedonian phalanx did for a period against the Roman legion. But these victories will grow more and more costly and less and less effective. The future of battle lies with the combat teams or 'battle groups' that can combine with, and at the same time act against, armour.

Some development in this direction has been shown by the British Army. During the campaign of November and December, 1941, in Libya mobile columns of all arms were formed, in a typically British and untheoretical way, on the initiative of Brigadier Jock Campbell, V.C. They were locally known as 'Jock columns.' Later, they seem to have been termed 'battle groups.' They were improvisations, and it is valuable to be able to improvise in war. But improvisation has its limits; the British Army was neither so trained nor so organised as to make the operation of forming and using these columns normal, standard, and well understood by all. This is one of the cases where to have a theory is in fact more 'practical' than to have none.

Armour and in-fighting go together. The tactics of the phalanx of Alexander were shock tactics. So were the tactics of the phalanx of tanks in the *Blitz* attack. They were shock tactics in the sense that the phalanx of tanks tried to get to close quarters with the enemy as rapidly as they could; but they did not use shock weapons such as the pike or bayonet. They used projectile weapons at relatively short ranges. It was by the concentration of their fire on a narrow front and at short ranges that they achieved a shock effect. And this effect was overwhelming against troops deployed in linear positions that could be directly approached and even overrun by the mass of tanks.

But when troops were deployed defensively in fortified towns and villages into which tanks could only penetrate at great risk, and in islands of resistance, 'hedgehogs' bristling with weapons in all directions and either naturally tank-proof or made proof against direct tank assault by the use of deep minefields, tanks could no longer employ shock tactics in the same way. The pendulum began to swing back from shock towards fire. The tanks had to use fire, and they had to be able to use fire effectively at any range up to the limit of direct visibility. Therefore, the standard German tank, on which they concentrated the productive capacities of Europe during 1940 and 1941, carried an artillery piece equivalent in size to a field gun. So did the typical medium Russian and American tanks produced in the same period. The typical British tank of the same weight, made in the same period, unfortunately, had no heavier armament than a two-pounder anti-tank gun, throwing a shell only one-seventh the weight of that of its rivals and opponents. This tragic mistake was made partly because of productive difficulties, partly because the officers and officials responsible for the design and production of tanks had no theoretical view as to their function or had a wrong theoretical view.

As far as there was any theoretical view of the function of tanks obvious in the British War Office and Ministry of Supply in 1940, it was the view that tanks were cavalry, to be used for reconnaissance and security, or the alternative view that they were anti-tank weapons with which to stop the enemy tanks. Our generals did not think of the armoured cavalry of history, the decisive arm of the Middle Ages; they thought of the light fox-hunting cavalry whose disappearance from the battlefield they so much regretted. (This light cavalry had never needed projectile weapons of any great range; the horse artillery built to accompany it was always light stuff.) They, therefore, asked for tanks with just enough weapons, as they thought, to protect themselves. And they actually called many of these tanks, during 1940 and later, 'cavalry tanks.' Their alternative theory was that tank should be used against tank; our armour should seek out and destroy the enemy armour. This is a completely different theory from that of the Germans. The German theory is that armour should be used against unarmoured men, and even against the weakest units and positions of these unarmoured men. The British theory was that our tanks should be used against the strongest enemy forces, their *Panzer* formations.

The idea that tanks should be used mainly against other tanks led, in British minds, to an astonishing misconception; British politicians and generals began to think of tanks as if they were battleships and lighter naval vessels. A fast medium tank became known as a 'cruiser' tank, and battles in the Western desert were described as if they were naval engagements. This is a misconception because naval vessels are designed for use as floating gun platforms and the guns have only one main purpose—to sink other ships.

Tanks are moving gun platforms on land, but the purpose of the guns they carry is to destroy enemy armed force. This armed force is not mainly available for destruction in the form of enemy armoured vehicles; it is mainly available for destruction in the form of unarmoured men and vehicles, and guns with little protection. This misconception is not responsible for the grotesque underarmament of our tanks; as a naval country we know that armoured vessels must carry big guns. But it is responsible, perhaps in conjunction with a misreading of Clausewitz, for the way our tanks were handled, as if they were fleets. The purpose of a battle fleet, in classical naval theory, is to bring the enemy battle fleet to action, destroy it, and then rule the seas. No such function could be carried out on land by an armoured force as soon as tank-proof islands of resistance were formed by the enemy. The 'battle fleet of tanks' was then reduced to cruising between these islands, which it could not rule, and it was soon found to lose heavily in the 'narrow waters' of these islands.

The misunderstanding of Clausewitz was a simple one, already exposed by some of the more intelligent theorists of warfare. Clausewitz laid down that the aim of battle was the destruction of the principal armed forces of the enemy. But he did not mean by that that battle should consist mainly, or even in part, of an attempt to close with the main body of the enemy in a head-on encounter. The confusion here is between the aim and the method: the aim is to destroy the enemy army, but the method cannot simply be defined as 'close with the enemy army and destroy it.' The main forces of the enemy can in some cases best be destroyed by indirect approach to them, by the baited attack that lures them to fight on the ground you have chosen, or by combining resistance and counterattack on the main battlefield with crippling diversions far from that field. Wellington and the guerrillas in Spain helped to weaken, and therefore to destroy, Napoleon's Grand Army near Moscow. It is childish to believe that military force can often be used as the dumb boxer uses his fists, without feint or stratagem, going straight for the enemy's main strength and hammering at it.

On the contrary, tank tactics are likely to develop in the future in such a way that attack is normally against the most vulnerable part of an enemy motorised infantry combat team, its supply columns and vehicle parks. In defence, tanks will be used for the counter-*Blitz,* the counterattack that does not go head-on against the enemy's armoured forces, but curls round behind them to catch the traffic jam of vehicles and troops coming up to their support. It is probable that the present tendency towards heavier tanks carrying heavier armament and armour will continue for a time; but a counter-tendency may begin and light machines may have more importance on the battlefield if guerrilla fighting and air-borne forces acquire the importance which I believe they will do. Only the lightest of tanks can be landed from the air; and the heavy tank is too greedy for fuel for it to be used as an auxiliary for guerrillas.

The *Blitzkrieg* can be considered as reaching its full development in the two years 1940-41; during 1942 it scored full successes only against obsolete methods of defence; against the modern methods of defence shown in Russia it may still score lesser successes at a greatly increasing cost. We have not yet reached the period when armour decreases in importance in warfare—a period parallel to that following the battle of Crécy. But we have reached the period when armour used alone decreases in importance, and auxiliary arms supporting and closely integrated with the armoured units become of increasing value and essential to the success of armour. We have entered the period like that before Crécy, the period when the crossbow and longbow are essential auxiliary arms. We know that in the past, when armoured forces have had to rely more and more on projectile auxiliaries, the time has come when the projectile of these auxiliaries eventually pierce the armour and sweep it off the battlefield. Are we in sight of such a period yet?

We are not yet in sight of this. The auxiliary arms are becoming more important, but they cannot yet so certainly meet and penetrate armour. They are, however, beginning to be quite dangerous to armour. The three auxiliary forces that matter most today in conjunction with the tank, and form part of the essential combat team used for a *Blitz* attack, are the air arm, mobile artillery, and mobile infantry. We cannot estimate when—if ever, in this war or in our lifetimes—one of these auxiliary arms can be developed to a level which 'negates' and cancels out the fighting value of armour. But we can see the probable line of development of each tending towards this end. This probable line of development is, for the air arm, the tank-busting plane; for artillery, the triple-purpose weapon; for infantry, tank-hunting along guerrilla lines and the use of high-explosive in great quantities in the form of mines and grenades.

The air arm had a very definite rôle to play in the theory and practice of the *Blitzkrieg;* its rôle is that of a flying artillery which can be concentrated very rapidly to open a path for tanks in the attack and to support attacking infantry. This rôle is completely different from long-range bombardment; an air force mainly built up to bomb an enemy country does not possess the right machines or the right training to form part of a combat team gaining tactical and strategical decisions on the ground. The typical machine used by the air force of the *Blitzkrieg* is a dive-bomber. This type of machine is not, as some have stated it to be, particularly valuable because of its accuracy. Its value lies in the fact that it comes close to its target, and can therefore distinguish this target under battle conditions more easily than a high-level bomber; and secondly, in the fact that it approaches its target in such a way that anti-aircraft fire against it is handicapped. The normal high-level bomber has to approach its target flying level or in a shallow dive and the anti-aircraft gunner below, after estimating its height, fuses his shells to burst at that height. The high-level bomber must also fly straight, in the approach to its target; the anti-aircraft guns can, therefore, be trained onto its line of flight. The dive-bomber, on the other hand, circles to spot its target and 'peels off' from its circle to approach the target from an unpredictable angle. It loses height when diving so rapidly that the anti-aircraft gunner is at a great disadvantage. And when an anti-aircraft barrage is being put up covering a certain area of sky, the diving machine gets through it more rapidly than the machine flying level. The dive-bomber also has considerably more moral effect on ground troops, until they get well used to it.

It seems almost certain for these reasons that a type of machine which normally dives towards its target will continue to be the most effective for cooperation with tanks and infantry, and for action against these ground forces. But if there is to be considerable development of planes as tank-busters, it is equally clear that the present types of dive-bomber are not so efficient as the types carrying a cannon of some size, or alternatively carrying a propelled bomb which can be aimed like a cannon shell. The Russians in their efforts to stop the *Blitzkreig* have developed both these types. The Americans have to some extent developed the former. It is more effective against tanks because tanks are small targets, which must be hit directly to secure a knockout and because the accuracy of a cannon shell or propelled bomb is naturally much greater than the accuracy of a bomb that drops under the influence of gravity, moved by its momentum and the winds. The Russian propelled bomb appears to be fired forward by some form of rocket, which may be a more effective method of propulsion for larger air-borne projectiles than discharge from a tube.

The other development of the air arm to be expected is the use of planes, more and more, as transport rather than as fighting vehicles. The Germans at this writing are said to employ sixteen per cent of their air force for this purpose. Their transport planes are used to carry parachutists, to land troops on captured aerodromes, to tow gliders that can land almost anywhere, and to take supplies to isolated forces infiltrating forward or holding islands of resistance surrounded by the enemy. While an airborne army may prove of very great strategic value, it may turn out that an almost equal value is to be gained from supply by 'the road through the air.' Supply questions have always hampered the more adventurous generals and have often prevented them from rapid advances otherwise practicable.

Captain Hugh Slater has suggested[2] the idea of an air-borne army consisting largely of armoured vehicles as the ultimate trend of modern mechanised war. While I agree to the extent that I have stated, that the plane is likely to become more valuable as transport than it has been in the past, I feel it likely (because of the limitations on weight that can be lifted) that the extension of function which will occur within increased air transport will be used to assist guerrilla forces rather than for the transport of heavy weapons and vehicles. In some cases the best support for guerrillas or for lightly armed forces, such as the Chinese armies, will be the transportation of heavy weapons and

[2] In *War into Europe.*

armoured fighting vehicles; but it is a far step from this to the transportation by air of complete armoured fighting units.

So long as the tactical pattern of the *Blitzkrieg* lasts, the primary fighting function of the air arm will be tactical and strategical support for, or struggle against, the mobile combat teams on the ground that are capable of decision. But when the *Blitzkrieg* is halted and its authors are forced—as they have been in Russia in 1942—to turn towards a tactical policy that they themselves describe as *aufreiben* (grinding, slicing, or grating), a policy of attrition in which they try to 'grind' through a strong web of defence, the air arm is likely to be the loosening agent by which war is made mobile again. And this development obviously will take the shape more of the transport plane and the glider than of the heavy bomber.

Second in our list of auxiliaries now capable of hampering or assisting the armoured force is mobile artillery. The two developments in this field already occurring and likely to increase in importance are the placing of guns on tracks so that they can go wherever tanks can go, and the development of the triple-purpose weapon.

The Germans had developed by 1940 an 'assault gun' consisting of a 105 millimetre (4.5 inch) gun mounted on the chassis of an obsolete tank. The gun carried a shield protecting the gunners from enemy fire coming from the direction in which the gun was directed. But the combination was not a tank, for this armoured shield was not carried round to the sides and rear of the machine. It was not a tank, but it was artillery assimilating itself to the tank. It is to be expected that this assimilation of artillery to the tank will continue, large mortars and gun howitzers up to perhaps the six-inch sixty-pounder will probably be put on tracks; others that remain on wheels will be so arranged for transportation that they are in position facing forward rather than to the rear while being towed. This gives the possibility of catching fleeting targets over open sights in the swift movement of mechanised battle.

A certain number of large tanks may in the future carry heavier armament than the three-inch piece of field artillery that is, at the time of writing, standard on most medium tanks in Germany, Russia, and America. But it is not likely that many 'real' tanks will be built carrying much heavier armament than this weapon. The Germans have armed some of their machines with 5.9-inch mortars, but these are mortars with a restricted range. The reason why it is unlikely that tanks as such will carry much heavier armament than the three-inch is that it is almost impossible to design armoured protection for a heavier gun and give the crew working it sufficient space to acquire a fairly high rate of fire. Three or four men can work behind the armoured shield of the assault gun. But to fit three or four men into a single turret, around the breech of a gun of some size, means that an inordinate weight of armour must be used, and even then the men will be cramped. Also from the tactical point of view there seems some waste involved in giving an engine to each separate piece of artillery; this is particularly true when a force is turning, perhaps temporarily, from the offensive to the defensive. It is not necessary to leave much transport within islands of resistance, but it may be necessary to leave guns; therefore, for certain purposes it is better that the prime mover which shifts the gun should be in the form of a tractor or 'dragon' rather than in the form of an engine built into the gun assembly. For these reasons it is unlikely that all artillery of field and medium types will be carried in tanks; but it is very likely that much of it will be carried on tracks, like the 'assault gun.'

The anti-tank gun as such will, I believe, become obsolete. It began in the period between the two wars as a light weapon usually of 20 millimetres (less than one inch). As a very rough and approximate rule you can say that a weapon of 20 millimetres has a good chance of piercing armour 20 millimetres thick; and a weapon of 50 millimetres armour 50 millimetres thick. The smallest size of anti-tank gun, therefore, could sometimes deal with armoured cars and light tanks with about an inch of armour plate round them, but even in 1937 in Spain it was clear that this was only possible at fairly close ranges. The 37-millimetre guns tried out in Spain proved capable of piercing the armour of many of the types of light tank used there; but the 45- and 47-millimetre guns were for more effective. It was clear by 1938 that heavier armour would come along and would require a heavier gun to oppose it. This I and others reported on returning from Spain, and I advocated publicly and in print the development of a gun similar to the German 88-millimetre triple-purpose gun.

This weapon is not, as it has recently been represented to be, an anti-aircraft gun converted in 1941 or 1942 to anti-tank uses. Whether or not, it was designed for all three purposes, I do not know; but it was being used by the summer of 1937 by the German Condor Legion as anti-tank, anti-aircraft, and field gun. It is of very great value to any commander to have a triple-purpose weapon of this type. As an anti-tank gun it is heavy enough to knock out any normal armour; but anti-tank gunners do not often have targets. They have to have their weapons in place and ready all the time, but enemy tanks seldom come their way and then only for a few minutes. Enemy aircraft pay rather more frequent visits, but move even more rapidly out of range. Between these brief periods of action the gun can serve as very effective field artillery.

It would have been natural for such a weapon to have been developed in Britain, since any British operations of war are likely to include landings from the sea, and it is much easier to land one triple-purpose weapon rather than three specialised weapons, each of which is useless or almost useless for the other purposes. Unluckily, the armed forces of Britain lived so continuously within watertight compartments, during peace and the first part of this war, that even the three sections of the Royal Artillery responsible for anti-tank, anti-aircraft, and field work scarcely seem aware of each other's existence. And if we possessed a triple-purpose weapon today—say our excellent 3.7-inch anti-aircraft gun, better than the German 88-millimetre, mounted and munitioned for anti-tank and field work as well as for its primary purpose—we should probably need a year or two of discussion before a decision could be reached as to which section of the Royal Artillery should man and command these weapons.

How much the theory of warfare affects the development and use of weapons can be seen from the story of our own 25-pounder gun-howitzer. This weapon receives well-deserved praise. It is in fact the finest field gun in the world—for a war like that of 1914-18. It is a gun of unrivalled accuracy and endurance for the laying of barrages and for fire against unseen stationary targets. It has, on the other hand, less value than the 18-pounder it replaces against moving targets over open sights. The 18-pounder's ammunition could be of the cartridge type; in other words, the ammunition would look like a much enlarged rifle cartridge, the whole of it in one piece, shell and cartridge together. Ammunition for the 25-pounder is normally, as is well known, in two parts, charge and shell. This has certain advantages, but with other points of design slows down the rate of fire to such an extent that the 25-pounder is less effective against tanks than the 18-pounder and much less than the German 88-millimetre is, or our 3.7-inch could be.

While artillery is being dealt with, it may be in place to suggest that shrapnel is likely to regain some of its former importance. The shrapnel shell is fused to burst in the air not far above the target, and the burst releases a considerable number of heavy lead bullets which scatter down over an area wider than that normally covered by blast or fragments from a high-explosive shell. In 1914 most field artillery ammunition was shrapnel, and the proportion of high-explosive was small. Then the armies went to ground, dug themselves into trenches. Shrapnel had not sufficient penetrative power to do much damage to men in trenches. It therefore decreased in importance and high-explosive increased (until gas shells became for field artillery equally or more important). War today is fought far less in trenches than was the case in the past. During the decisive moment in many engagements the targets for artillery are either infantry in trucks or infantry scattering out from these trucks, or supply convoys or other vulnerable vehicles such as tank transporters. I believe it may be found that shrapnel, because of the area over which it is lethal, is a better weapon against such targets than high-explosive. And in modern defence, when the main aim is often to keep enemy infantry from following up their tanks, I am certain that a number of field guns or triple-purpose guns firing shrapnel from forward islands of resistance is likely to delay the enemy infantry more than the same number of guns firing high-explosive.

Where, as in Russia, towns are strongly held, heavy artillery will come back into the picture. The Germans are already using a 16-inch howitzer and a 24-inch railway gun. But the main shape of war will remain too mobile for these monstrosities.

It is impossible to forecast with any certainty the effect of the use of poison gas on modern tactics. For the main defensive purpose stated, that of separating the attacking infantry from their tanks, persistent gas would seem to have some value, and to that extent it might slow up the process of modern attack and tend towards the negation of the *Blitzkrieg*. On the other hand, it might prove a valuable offensive weapon against islands of resistance so well fortified that projectiles have little effect upon them; it might have an even greater effect against guerrillas necessarily lightly equipped, and has been used by the Japanese extensively against Chinese armies and guerrillas who lack gas masks. The armoured vehicle can be made proof against gas, and so can the aeroplane; probably the effect of gas during the first period of its use in this war, if it is used at all, will be mainly to hamper or help in destroying those forces which are so conservative in equipment and tactics that they do not quickly make tanks, planes, and troop-carrying vehicles gas-proof. The use of gas spray from the air may have an effect on civilian populations in areas where government propaganda has made gas into a terrifying neurosis; but its actual destructive value is small. Gas has not so far been used in this war on a large scale by our enemies because we possessed, until 1942, better facilities for making poisons and most of the rubber of the world. During 1942 we lost ninety per cent of the world's crude-rubber resources, and our enemies are now in a better position than we are to 'armour' themselves against gas. It would be wise, therefore, for the question of the effect of gas on modern tactics to be more thoroughly studied. For example, as our equipment stands now, it is not clear that fighter aeroplanes could be worked from aerodromes heavily sprayed with heavy concentrations of persistent gas.

The main processes in the development of modern infantry are three: motorisation and close linking with armour; development of tank-hunting and of defences against tanks; and approximation to guerrilla methods and tactics. Motorisation has already gone so far that considerable forces can move at the speed of tanks; the weakness of these forces in action is that enemy machine-gun fire can make them dismount from their vehicles and can check their pace to that of men crawling. The Russians, trying to develop a close integration of tanks and infantry, have pulled armoured sledges of infantry behind their tanks on snowy ground, and have carried small parties of machine-gunners and automatic riflemen crouching on the actual tanks themselves. It seems likely there will be further development of both these ideas; various types of armoured infantry carriers will be tried out, and some form of bullet-proof shield behind the normal tank turret will make it possible for tanks to 'ferry' infantry forward at a rapid pace.

Infantry against tanks has not yet shown its full powers. This may be due to a theoretical misunderstanding of the nature of the job. Infantry has been given projectile weapons of various sorts, anti-tank rifles and light anti-tank guns, as its main weapons for use against tanks. I repeat that armour and in-fighting have always gone together; and I believe the theoretical conclusion from this is that infantry should be trained to tackle tanks mainly at extremely close ranges. They can do so only if trained to be practically invisible to tanks, which necessarily have restricted vision, at such ranges. And their main weapon against armour at such ranges is high-explosive, either in the form of a heavy anti-tank grenade, in the form of the anti-tank mine, or in the form of some relatively heavy projectile which gets its effect on the tank by high-explosive blast rather than by penetration of the armour due to high muzzle velocity. The solid bullet fired by the anti-tank rifle, or the solid shell fired by the light antitank gun, can only get its effect if it penetrates the armour and hits a vital spot; but high-explosive blast can much more easily destroy tracks or running gear or blow a considerable hole in the armour. The bullet or solid shell must be propelled at a high speed; the high-explosive projectile can be thrown by hand or projected relatively slowly. Against some types of tank, fire is still effective; any tank must take in air and where air goes in flame can go in.

Armour in the past has been conquered, as at Crécy, by projectile auxiliaries. It may be conquered again by such auxiliaries, plane or gun. But it may also be conquered by something approximating to shock tactics—by the shock or blast of high-explosive, a new form of shock that could not be used in the past.

Men make the most complicated and costly weapons in order to cause an explosion near the enemy—great guns, bombing planes, or torpedoes. And then they find against a dispersed or armoured enemy that only a small proportion of their ingenious and powerful projectiles secure any effect whatever. An infantry hidden either by camouflage and stillness or by smoke or by darkness can deliver explosives 'by hand' and are more likely to see that it gets to the right address. This new and—to some officers—rather frightening function of infantry is of course not in fact entirely new: the tank-hunters of today and tomorrow are only the modern equivalents of the grenadiers of the seventeenth century. Like those grenadiers, they must be a picked and courageous infantry; but their job is possible and has already been done to some extent by men in Spain and Russia.

In a period dominated by armour and mobility it is impossible for infantry to protect themselves on the battlefield mainly by entrenchment. Their chief protection becomes invisibility, not only when enemy tanks are among them, but when enemy planes are over them. That is the first reason why most of the methods and tactics of modern infantry will progressively be approximated to those of guerrillas. A guerrilla force is essentially invisible; it strikes from the dark, the jungle, the city's back alleys, or the difficult hills, and it retires or scatters to disappear immediately after it has struck its blow. All the conditions of modern tactics make it possible for a lively light infantry to fight in this way; swift and deep advances by mechanised and motorised forces, the swirl and ebb of attack and counter-attack through narrow channels between islands of resistance, have split up battle into a greater number of isolated small engagements, in which the infantry unit that knows how to be as independent and as unpredictable as a guerrilla force has enormous opportunities. If infantry is considered, in such a battle, only as a defensive force against other infantry or as moppers-up cleaning away the debris after an armoured attack has gone through, it cannot be fully integrated with the combat team of tanks and planes to which it is only an appendage or a target. But if, on the other hand, infantry plays its own and active part in the battle, in defence dangerous vermin hard to dig out of the seams of the soil, and in attack a stinging swarm that appears out of nowhere and vanishes as quickly as it appears—then infantry can once again become the most powerful factor in the combination that makes up an army.

Such an infantry will use smoke cover to a much greater extent than is normal at, present. Infantry commanders of the conservative sort worry mainly about their own control over their men; smoke interferes with this control and units unaccustomed to it lose direction when moving through smoke. But continuous control over small units by commanders behind those units is no longer possible under any conditions of modern battle; and smoke or darkness are the only conditions which meet the theoretical necessity that I have stated—the necessity for infantry to rely for protection on invisibility rather than entrenchment.

It was noticeable during the Japanese campaign in Malaya that the normal Japanese advance would cease by about three in the afternoon; the Japanese soldiers were then fed and rested until midnight or soon after, when their main infiltration movement would begin again. Using darkness to pass through our lines and encircle our units, they would be so placed at dawn that their fire could command not only our positions, from all angles, but also all ways of retreat from those positions. This is the typical technique of the guerrilla, and was doubtless learned by the Japanese from the Chinese forces, which have carried guerrilla tactics and the approximation of infantry to guerrillas to as high a level of development as the Russians.

Infantry have far more street-fighting to do, in the years of the *Blitzkrieg* and in the subsequent years that now—I suggest—are going to be shaped by a clash between the *Blitzkrieg* and even newer ideas of war. The *Blitz* attack aims at rapid irruption and then even more rapid movement, beyond the breaches created, to form the *Kessel* or cauldron. Much of this movement occurs on roads; where roads cross, there are towns and villages; if these are held by a determined infantry, the *Blitz* is slowed down and the armoured formations are split up, channelled into smaller and smaller units, and cut off from truck-borne troops and supplies following them.

Built-up areas in the last war used to be flattened by artillery, at great cost in time and shells. In a typical *Blitz* attack they cannot be flattened; there is not enough time. They must be stormed. And they cannot be stormed by tanks. Tanks in streets are at a serious disadvantage. They cannot carry enough shells to destroy all the houses on each side of the streets. They cannot clean defending infantry from the rubble of ruined buildings, which gives this infantry as good or better cover than untouched walls and windows. A tank in a street is in a defile with enemy infantry at short grenade range on each side of it, and therefore it is constantly in danger.

During street-fighting, bombers are at a disadvantage; they cannot find their targets. So street-fighting is mainly infantry work; it is usually slow work; and the defenders have advantages over the attackers. When met by a defence that holds the built-up areas, and therefore the road junctions, a *Blitz* force attacking must bring up its infantry and guns. The Russians held their towns; that is why the *Panzer* divisions, and the *Blitzkrieg* itself, had to change and slow down in Russia. When such a defence is determined and skilful, as at Sebastopol, the whole town may have to be knocked down before it can be captured. This takes months; and the Germans had to waste precious months of spring and early summer on it in 1942. Where, on the other hand, defences round a town are linear—as at Tobruk in 1942—the Germans break through these defences on a narrow front, drive straight to the centre of the built-up area, and work out from there to take perimeter defences from the rear.

Street-fighting and guerrilla fighting are linked in method and aim, as ways of resistance that can be effective against the *Blitzkrieg*. Both have been taught, in Britain, by the school of military thought that began by teaching these methods of fighting to the Home Guard at the Osterley Park School in 1940.

The clearest proof that street-fighting can hold up the *Blitzkrieg* is the siege of Stalingrad, which began after the text of this book was completed. At the moment of writing, this siege continues; it is the biggest battle of its sort that has ever occurred. Tanks, planes, heavy guns, and scores of infantry divisions have hammered at the city. It is not a Verdun, for at Verdun the Germans never penetrated into the built-up area. The distinguishing characteristic of this fighting is that it is the defence of the built-up area by street-fighting. The city is now being pulverised, as Sebastopol was; but it is built on softer soil than most of Sebastopol, and therefore the larger shells and bombs make craters from which the defence can be continued. There will be more battles of the shape of Stalingrad in the future, and fewer campaigns of the shape of Singapore—as soon as all our forces have learned street-fighting and the closely connected methods of guerrilla war.

Both Russians and Chinese have been able to maintain large and effective forces within areas nominally occupied by their enemies. The whole aim of modern techniques of war is to get men and weapons to effective points behind the enemy's main positions. It is with this aim that the *Blitzkrieg* is designed, and very costly armoured machines made. It is with this aim that bombers and airborne armies are built; with this aim the parachutists come down. The guerrilla is 'there already'; he has his weapons at the point where the enemy is weakest. He strikes against enemy material where that material is stored or is in, process of transport and therefore cannot swiftly be brought into action, rather than against the same material deployed in the enemy's main positions and ready for action. The guerrilla also strikes at morale where morale is weakest, behind the picked units and the men securely armoured. A guerrilla force cannot dispose of the immense amounts of ammunition and other supplies that a more regular force in contact with its base can possess. Therefore, it wastes far less ammunition; in its cloak of invisibility it gets to close quarters with the enemy and restores simplicity to battle.

The combat team that makes up the decisive force of the *Blitz* type of attack is enormously powerful; but behind it must come the gasoline trucks and the supply convoys, a great traffic jam of vehicles, mobile workshops, staff cars, and all the rest. The aim of modern tactics is to use effective force against these soft parts of the enemy organism. A *Blitz* force is like a man with head and trunk well armoured, but with no protection below the waist. It is unnecessary for any real soldier that I should complete this paragraph.

The pattern of warfare that can make the *Blitzkrieg* obsolete, the emerging pattern of today, is in my belief that of the Peoples' War. This is a pattern of warfare which treats as principal the active linking of an armed population with an offensive striking force. Where possible this striking force will be patterned on and developed from that of the *Blitzkrieg;* it will have tanks and planes and triple-purpose artillery and truck-borne infantry and all the paraphernalia of mechanised war. But the weapons of the armed population will be cheap and simple to make; tommy-guns, raw explosives for mines and grenades, machine rifles, and the like. Civilian transport and civilian radio sets will help to link these forces to each other and to the striking force; they will use the cities as their hiding-places as well as the hills. They will fight in the streets as well as in the fields. Guerrilla forces made from an armed population cannot be expected to be decisive without the backing of a striking force; the Spanish guerrillas could not defeat Napoleon's armies, though they could drain the strength of those armies. Only when Wellington's striking force was in play could the game be won. But the existence and work of the guerrillas make it possible for a relatively small striking force to defeat much more powerful armies.

The methods of the Peoples' War have until 1942 only been used on the strategic defensive. By these methods the Chinese have resisted for five years the attack of an immensely more powerful enemy, supplied for almost all these five years by all the resources of the industrial democracies. These methods have had to form in Britain a force, the Home Guard, that could be made capable of taking most of the duties of the defence of this country upon its shoulders, so that most of the regular troops in Britain could be used as a striking force on the Continent. In Russia the guerrillas have played not only an heroic part, but a most effective part in the first year of 'the Russian glory.' But 'you ain't seen nothin' yet'; when the same methods are developed for the strategic offensive against Fascism, the Peoples' War will seem throughout Europe more like an explosion than a campaign.

I suggested towards the beginning of this book that the underlying reasons for any revolution in the technique of warfare normally lie somewhat outside the developments inherent within warfare itself; such changes come when the peoples who make up a nation or several nations express themselves in a democratic or popular or revolutionary way. The democracy of the Greeks, of the 'barbarians' who broke the legion, Charlemagne's nation-state, the yeoman independence of the archers at Crécy, the released energies of American, French, Soviet, and Nazi revolutions—all these, though difficult to equate or measure beside each other, have been the underlying reasons for revolutions in the technique of war. If my thesis is correct and the *Blitzkrieg* is to be replaced by the Peoples' War, by a combination of guerrilla and mechanised striking force, this revolution in warfare will be caused by and will take the shape of a popular anti-Fascist revolution throughout Europe and beyond Europe. To that, the forces working and fighting against Fascism in America or Russia, in the British Empire or China or ruined Europe, will all contribute in their own way. But no contribution can be made by those who hold to old ways of fighting, as they hold to old ways of living, because change seems alien and unpleasant and threatening to them. Change in technique, in tactics and strategy and supply and equipment, transport and training, and every aspect of warfare—change is the only law that persists throughout warfare. If we are to survive and be victorious, we must learn the ways of change.

ABOUT THE AUTHOR

Tom Wintringham (1898-1949) graduated from Oxford after finishing service during World War 1 as mechanic and despatch for the Royal Flying Corps. He became involved in socialist politics and journalism, eventually becoming involved in the fighting during the Spanish Civil War. Returning from Spain, he recognized the threat of Axis aggression, and began campaigning for the creation of what would become the Home Guard in the United Kingdom. Because of his politics, Wintringham was not accepted into the British Army, but the Home Guard continued its useful purpose even after he resigned.

ADDENDUM

ANCIENT AND MODERN ARTILLERY

Harper's New Monthly Magazine, March 1855

In few things have men displayed so much ingenuity as in devising and perfecting implements for destroying each other. The necessities of the chase, indeed, demanded projectile weapons; and Nimrod, "the mighty hunter before the Lord," must have had some means of attacking game at a distance greater than he could hurl a stone or cast a spear. When the hunter of beasts became a hunter of men, the same weapons would come into play, and new ones would be brought into requisition. In point of fact, war, rather than the chase, has led to the invention of projectiles.

The sling being the most simple and obvious, was undoubtedly the earliest instrument for casting missiles. It was but increasing the momentum of the stone by augmenting the circumference of the circle around which it was whirled. Slingers constituted the great body of the light-armed troops of antiquity. The weapon was easily constructed, and the missiles adapted to it abounded everywhere. Every tent which contained a bit of leather was an armory. Every brook course, with its smooth water-worn stones, was a magazine abundantly stored. There was little room for improvement in the construction of the sling. The earliest were, in all essential respects, as perfect as the latest. Those found in the Egyptian tombs do not differ from those used three thousand years later. The only advance made was in the employment of leaden bullets in place of the smooth stones with which the Hebrew youth slew the Philistine giant. It is not a little singular that these bullets were made of an almond-shape, very like the conical balls which modern science has shown to be preferable to the round ones so long employed. Among the Greeks these bullets not unfrequently bore some motto or inscription. Every bullet literally had its billet. A very common one was, "Take this!"—an invitation wholly superfluous to the person who chanced to be hit.

The range of the sling was great enough to make it a very formidable weapon, though skill in its use could be acquired only by early training and long practice. The inhabitants of the Balearic Islands had a reputation as marksmen akin to that enjoyed by our "Kentucky riflemen." This proficiency was the result of early training, the mothers of the young slingers being accustomed to suspend the food of their sons from the branch of a tree, compelling them to bring it down with the sling, or go hungry. With them it was, "No hit, no dinner."

SLINGER.

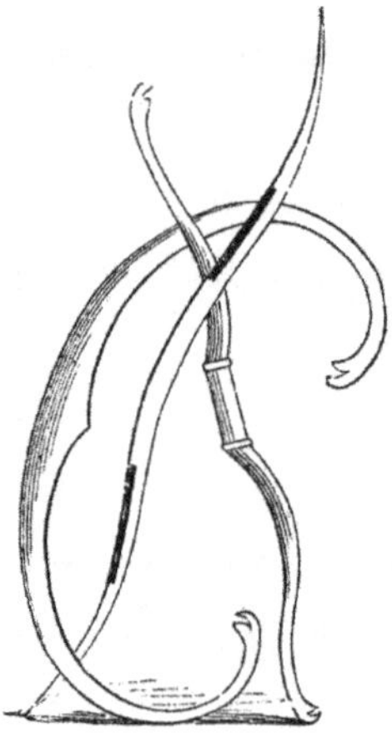

ANCIENT BOWS.

Next after the sling came the bow. This was still more widely diffused, owing to its greater accuracy. The bows of various nations differed greatly from each other. That of the Scythians was shaped like our letter C, the ancient form of the Greek *sigma*. Hence the young Greek was told to remember the form of that letter, "because it was like a Scythian bow," just as among us the figure of the letter B is impressed upon the mind of the rustic aspirant for alphabetical knowledge, by calling attention to the fact that it "looks like an ox-yoke." The bow used by the Tartars, the descendants of the Scythians, still retains this shape. As they fight principally upon horseback, they hold the bow vertically, instead of horizontally like other nations. The neck of the horse is thus prevented from interfering with the action of the bow.

The Greek bow was short, not exceeding three or four feet in length. But as it was very stout, considerable force was required to bend it. In using it, the archer dropped upon one knee, bracing himself so as to gain a firmer position. This attitude is shown in the annexed outline of an ancient statue. The bow itself is not represented; but the position of the hands shows that the arrow was drawn to the breast, instead of back to the ear. The Greek bow was originally made of two horns of a species of wild goat, united at the base by a metallic band forming the handle. Of whatever material it was afterward constituted, this form was still retained. The double curvature, with the straight intervening handle, still showed its origin. The Romans copied their bows, as well as many other things, from the Greeks.

GREEK ARCHER.

The Egyptians were celebrated as archers. Their bows bore a close resemblance, both in form and length, to the famous English long-bow. Specimens now extant, taken from the tombs at Thebes, might pass for the very weapons borne by Robin Hood and the merry archers of Sherwood forest. Their arrows also rivaled in length the cloth-yard shafts of the English archers. Compared with the long Egyptian bow, that of the Greeks was a very clumsy, inefficient weapon. It may seem strange that the Greeks and Romans should never have thought of the obvious expedient of adding to the power of their bow by increasing its length. But there was something in the weapon not adapted to their genius. They trusted to hand-to-hand fighting, rather than to missiles. They had that bull-dog propensity that has made the bayonet the favorite weapon of the English. The archers in their armies belonged almost exclusively to the auxiliary troops, for the bow was an Asiatic rather than a European weapon. The Orientals could never stand before the onset of the serried spears of the Greek phalanx, or the charge of the heavy pilum and short cut-and-thrust sword of the Roman legion.

The nations of antiquity possessed nothing answering to our modern field artillery. But some ordnance was absolutely essential for attacking fortified places. The most obvious instrument for overthrowing walls and bursting in gates was the battering-ram. In its earliest form it was simply a huge beam, borne in the brawny arms of the soldiers, and thrust by direct force against the walls or gate. To add a metallic head to the beam, to suspend it by chains from a support, and to protect those who used it by a movable tower or other defense, were all the essential improvements of which this simple instrument was capable. When of the enormous size of which it was sometimes made, the ram was a very formidable implement, comparing in some respects not unfavorably with our heaviest siege artillery. A French mathematician has calculated that a ram weighing two tons, moved by the force of a thousand men, gave a blow equal to that of a 36-pound shot, fired point-blank. This size was often far exceeded. We read of those which weighed forty or fifty tons, requiring 1500 men to manage them effectively. Nothing less firm than a solid pyramid could long sustain the shock of such an implement fairly brought against it.

The obvious defects of the battering-ram were the exposed situation of those who used it, working, as they necessarily must, directly exposed to the assaults of the besieged; the immense force necessary to manage it; and the difficulty of transporting it from place to place, and establishing it in position. One employed by Vespasian,

BATTERING-RAM.

and by no means the largest of which we have accounts, required for its transportation one hundred and fifty yoke of oxen, or three hundred pairs of horses and mules.

The battering-ram, moreover, was effective only against the defenses of a place, inflicting no direct injury upon the defenders. To effect this latter purpose, the ancients invented a great variety of engines for hurling huge stones and immense darts and javelins, or even beams of considerable size. Though differing widely in construction, these may all be reduced to two classes, as far as their principle of operation is concerned.

INFERNAL MACHINE.

The first class is simply a bow of great size, furnished with a winch or other machinery for bending it, and a rest for sustaining the rock or bolt to be hurled. This principle was brought into use in an infinite variety of forms, and specific names were given to each. The bow was placed horizontally or vertically; it had one arm or two, and was made of wood or metal. One form reminds us of the "infernal machine" by which it was attempted to assassinate Louis Philippe. A number of arrows were arranged side by side upon a support. A stout elastic board, placed perpendicularly, was firmly secured at the lower end, while the upper end was bent back by a winch. When let go, the board sprung back against the arrows, discharging them all at once.

The other class of engines derived their power from the elasticity of twisted fibres. Such an engine was called a *tormentum,* from the Latin *torqueo,* "to twist"—and not, as might appear to the mere English reader, from its tormenting the enemy. A common wood-saw furnishes a perfect illustration of their principle of construction. Let any one draw back the slip of wood by which the cord is twisted, and then let it fly back against his knuckles; he will need no further proof of elastic force of twisted fibres. Increase the number of cords, make the frame of suitable strength and form, and provide an appropriate support for the missile, and we have the ancient *tormentum.* In some the stone to be thrown was placed in a cavity at the extremity of the lever; the action of throwing then resembled that by which a stone is flung by the arm.

The names *catapulta* and *ballista* were applied indifferently to both species of engines; the former denoting those intended for throwing darts, the latter those for hurling stones. The shape given to each depended much upon the purpose for which it was designed; the ballista being usually square, and the catapulta oblong. Hence the boast of the "shoulder-hitter" in the old Latin comedy; "My fist is a ballista, my lower arm a catapulta, and my upper arm a battering-ram."

It will be observed that *elasticity* is the power made available in both these species of engines. In the one case it is the elasticity of wood or metals; in the other that of twisted fibres. It is the same force, acting under different conditions, that is used in modern artillery. The explosive power of gunpowder arises from the elasticity of the gases suddenly evolved in its rapid combustion. The volume of the gases thus produced is two thousand times that of the powder employed. It is difficult to measure the absolute expansive force of these. Count Rumford filled a cavity in an iron cylinder with twenty-eight grains of gunpowder.

TORMENTUM.

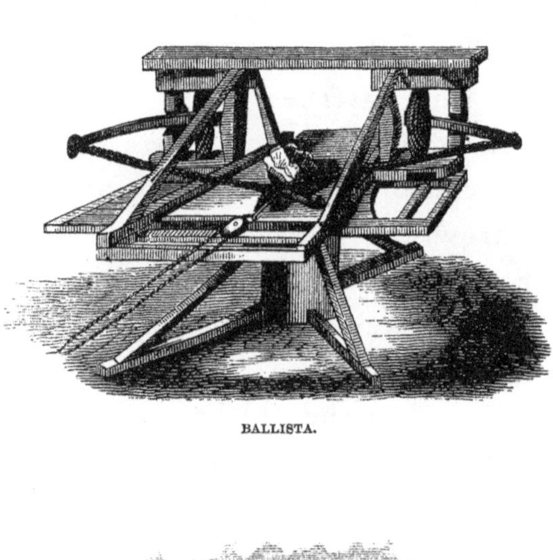

BALLISTA.

CATAPULTA.

In exploding, it tore asunder the iron, which would have resisted a strain of 400,000 pounds applied at no greater mechanical advantage. Here, as in the case of steam, we see that the elasticity of gases exceeds almost infinitely that of any solid bodies.

The application of gunpowder wrought an entire change in the whole system of warlike engines. The explosive power of this compound had been familiar long before it was applied to this purpose. It had been known in the East, and used in the construction of fireworks, from time immemorial. Roger Bacon was acquainted with it as early as 1219. In 1280 the monk Barthold Schwartz appears to have pointed out its applicability to warlike engines. It was not long before the idea was carried into execution. Cannon were certainly used in France as early as 1328. The presence of a number of pieces of cannon at the battle of Cressy, in 1346, proves that they were not an absolutely new invention then, as has been assumed. An army circumstanced as was that of Edward III is in no condition to try experiments with new weapons upon a battle-field.

The new invention was improved by slow degrees. Yet the range of even the rude guns first fabricated so far exceeded that of the catapulta and ballista, as to call for the most strenuous efforts for their improvement. The main obstacle to this was the low state of the mechanic arts. Milton's description of the artillery of the rebel angels applies exactly to the guns first made. They were mere logs of wood hollowed out. The wooden tube was then strengthened by iron bars and hoops; and at a later period the bore was lined with iron. During the Thirty Years' War, Gustavus Adolphus had a number of guns made much more portable than any that had before been known. To preserve them, they were inclosed in leather cases. This is probably the origin of the absurd story that has passed from author to author, of cannon having been sometimes made of leather.

At length guns were cast in one piece. At first the bore was formed in casting. An iron rod covered with clay was inserted in the mould, which was withdrawn after the casting, leaving a hollow tube. It soon appeared that the bore thus produced was not perfectly accurate; besides that the interior was always honey-combed by the air-bubbles escaping from the molten metal, which weakened the piece. At present all cannon are cast solid, the bore being produced by drilling. In boring, the drill is stationary, the gun being made to revolve by powerful machinery.

It would be superfluous to enumerate the successive changes made in the form of artillery. The main points to be gained were to establish the best ratio between the length of the piece and the size of the bore; and to secure the greatest available strength with the least amount of metal. As the greatest force of the explosion is felt at the place where it first takes place, the breech was made considerably thicker than any other part. The full explosive power of the charge is apparent only when it is closely confined, as in Rumford's experiment. The bottom of the bore, where the powder is placed, was accordingly made smaller than the remainder, which was large enough to admit the ball. This diminished bore constitutes the "chambered breech," which is now applied to small arms as well as cannon.

Attention was also directed to the gun-carriages, in order to construct one which should combine strength, lightness, and facility of movement. In modern field-pieces, the gun rests only upon the hind-wheels, the fore-wheels or "limbers" being detached when the piece is fired. The stout side-pieces, or trails, resting on the ground, give a firm position to the gun. To "unlimber" is to detach the fore-wheels from the carriage, leaving the trails to rest upon the ground. The limber also serves as a vehicle for transporting some of the most necessary munitions and a portion of the gunners. The 9-pounder brass gun is the favorite piece of field artillery in the English service, those of larger calibre being too heavy to be transported with facility over rough ground. The piece itself weighs 13 cwt. Including gun, carriage, limber, 32 rounds of ammunition, and the necessary stores, it weighs 38 ½ cwt., and can be drawn for a few hundred yards by six horses at a gallop, so as to bring it speedily into position. As now organized in the Eastern war, an English field battery of four 9-pounders and two 24-pounder howitzers has in attendance fourteen other carriages, served by 20 officers, commissioned and non-commissioned, 168 gunners, drivers, etc., and 170 horses.

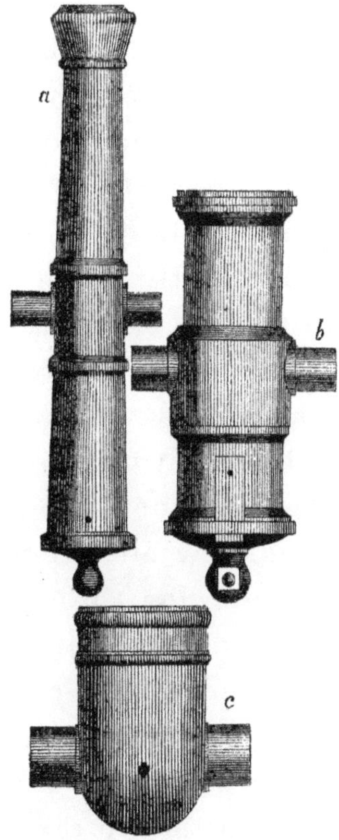

CANNON, HOWITZER, MORTAR.

As now constituted, artillery may be divided into three classes: cannon (*a*), howitzers (*b*), and mortars (*c*), distinguished by their different proportions. In field guns the length is from sixteen to twenty-one times the diameter of the bore. Naval and siege guns are made somewhat longer, in order that the muzzle may project beyond the sides of the ship or the embankments from which they are fired, in order that they may not be injured by the concussion. Mortars are very short, with a large bore; their length is three or four times their calibre. Howitzers are a medium between the other two classes; their length being six or eight times their calibre. Each of these guns is specially adapted to a particular kind of projectile. The calibre of cannon is indicated by the weight of the ball which it carries; that of mortars by the diameter of the bore; either method is used with respect to howitzers. The 5 ½-inch howitzer carries a stone ball weighing seven pounds; thus a 5 ½-inch howitzer and a 7-pounder howitzer denote the same piece. The hollow iron ball of the same size weighs twice as much.

For a long time solid round balls, at first of stone, afterward of iron, were the only projectiles discharged by artillery. For battering down walls, the solid ball has the advantage over all others. But when directed against a body of men its efficient range is limited to the direct line of its flight. If the enemy were drawn up in a single line, no ball could kill more than a single man, while the chances would be greatly against its hitting even that one. A number of small shot, directed against a body of men, are more efficient than one large one. To meet this condition grape and cannister shot are employed.

Grape shot are a number of balls slightly fastened together around an iron spindle, in a form somewhat like a cluster of grapes. A cannister shot in shape is precisely like the tin cases used for containing preserved meats. But instead of appetizing delicacies, it is filled with hard iron balls. The design of grape and cannister shot is the same. The rapid flight of the mass through the air bursts the packages, and the balls scatter wide, plowing a broad furrow through the opposing ranks. Now, as a half-pound ball will kill a man as effectually as one of fifty pounds, and as one is just as likely to hit as the other, we may consider the efficiency of grape and cannister shot to exceed that of a solid ball just in proportion to the number of bullets they contain. Hence against troops in the

FIELD PIECE BROUGHT INTO ACTION.

MORTAR PRACTICE.

open field, except at a very long range, grape and cannister have superseded solid shot.

Various forms have been tried for shot. There have been, for example, cylindrical, oblong, pine-apple, chain, and bar shot. These last are simply two round balls joined together by a chain or iron rod. But they have gone almost out of use; though in the recent naval attack upon Sebastopol, the Russians did great damage to the rigging of the vessels of the Allies by the use of chain shot. It has been found that when a ball passes through an object with a great momentum, it makes a clean smooth hole of just its own size. If the momentum is less, a large ragged hole is produced. In naval warfare the object is quite as much to damage the enemy's vessel as to kill his men. In order to diminish the momentum of the balls, they have been lightened, either by making them of stone or of iron hollow. The guns for discharging these shot were usually made with a bore larger in proportion to their length than common cannon. Such pieces, as well as the balls shot from them, were called carronades. It was found, however, that the advantage thus gained was more than neutralized by the inferior range of the carronades. Thus during our late war with Great Britain, our inferior fleet on Lake Ontario was saved from destruction by the British vessels being armed chiefly with carronades, while ours bore long guns carrying solid shot. Having the wind of the enemy, our fleet could keep beyond the range of their carronades, peppering them at leisure, and in almost perfect security. "We remained in this mortifying condition for six hours," says the British commander, "without being able to return a shot."

For attacking towns the red-hot shot is probably the most destructive projectile yet invented. To the horrors of bombardment it adds those of conflagration. At first sight it would seem the height of folly to thrust a red-hot mass of iron within an inch or two of a charge of gunpowder. The artilleryman would seem to stand in more peril than any one else. But the hazard is really very slight. The powder is inclosed in a stout flannel cartridge, and two thick hempen waddings, one wet, the other dry, are interposed between the ball and the powder. Still, a red-hot ball is not a very convenient thing to handle, since it must be done by means of tongs, and at great mechanical disadvantage. Hence red-hot shot of more than two-and-thirty pounds have rarely been used. At the recent bombardment of Odessa, however, it is said that red-hot shot were thrown from guns of the largest calibre.

Shells are probably the most terrible arm of modern warfare. A shell of the simplest form is a hollow ball of iron, filled with gunpowder and other combustible matter. A fuse communicates, through a hole in the side, with the enclosed powder. The fuse is ignited by the firing of the gun, its length being so calculated that it may last till the shell has just reached its mark. The shell is burst by the explosion of the powder within, and its fragments scattered in every direction.

Such is the simple bomb-shell—a missile destructive enough, one would think, to satisfy the most blood-thirsty mind. But it must yield the palm to the Shrapnel-shell, which is stuffed with both balls and powder. It thus combines in itself the destructive properties of the solid ball, the cannister shot, and the. shell. Its range is nearly as great as that of the first, while it has the diffused action of the two last.

Attempts have been made at various times to cause shells to explode by the concussion of striking their mark; for it is difficult to calculate with perfect accuracy the proper length of the fuse to burn just the right time; and if the explosion takes place a few seconds too soon, the shell is harmless. But none of the attempts have as yet been proved satisfactory, by actual use, though it is said the secret is in possession of both the French and English governments. This, however, is still doubtful. So also is the reported invention of asphyxiated shells, filled with a composition that when burned produces immense volumes of a gas fatal to life.

Cannon and howitzers, as now used, throw both shot and shells. A Paixhan gun is simply a howitzer or cannon of enormous calibre, capable of taking in a large shell. Such was the great gun, called by a ghastly pun on its name, "The Peacemaker," the explosion of which on board the *Princeton* a few years since, was so disastrous. Mortars are used only for throwing shells. There is. this further peculiarity about them. The shell is not aimed directly at the mark, but is shot upward, in order that it may in falling descend upon its object. Thus a shell is thrown clean over the walls of a fortress, and falls into its midst. The mortar, therefore, is fired at an angle of 45 degrees, being the angle which gives the ball the greatest range.

For many years great attention has been paid by military engineers to the rockets invented by Colonel Congreve, and high anticipations were at one time entertained of their efficiency. It was supposed that they would work an entire change in this arm of military service. Though these anticipations have been only partially realized, the rocket is now introduced as a useful auxiliary into siege trains. In external appearance the Congreve rocket differs little from the ordinary signal rocket. It is, however, much larger, and the case is made of iron. As the rocket always goes head-on, it is easy to cause it to explode by the shock of its contact in striking its mark. It is fired from a rest, so arranged as to give direction to its flight. The great defect in the rocket, which has never been fully obviated, is the uncertainty of its aim. Their use is almost wholly confined to siege purposes. For setting fire to towns they have been found very efficacious, as a large amount of incendiary material is easily attached to them.

The application of gunpowder to small arms was much more slow than to artillery. The first steps were simply in the direction of lightening the pieces to facilitate transport. The carriage was then dispensed with, and they were mounted upon a tripod, like a telescope. Next came what were called wall-pieces. They had no stand, but were still too heavy to be discharged from the arm. The muzzle was rested upon the wall, and the piece steadied by being brought to the shoulder. To avoid the "kicking" of so heavily loaded a piece, the muzzle had a projection which was hooked over the wall, so as to receive the shock of the recoil. This was only adapted to the defense of walled towns. It could not be used in the field.

The construction of the *harquebuse* was a very decided step in advance. This was light enough to be transported on the shoulder, but too heavy to be aimed without a rest. This rest was at first attached to the piece; but was

FIRING ROCKETS.

subsequently detached, and carried sometimes by the harquebusier himself, and sometimes by an attendant. It was a stout staff, shod with iron, and having a forked top, in which to rest the gun.

Up to this time the piece was discharged by a slow match. As long as the rest was employed, the gunner had always a hand at liberty to manage the match. But when, in process of time, the piece was so far lightened that it might be fired at arm's length, this mode of discharge caused much embarrassment. This led to the invention of gun-locks. The earlier form was that of a simple dog to hold the slow-match, connected with a trigger, by pulling

ANCIENT DEFENSIVE WARFARE.

which the match was brought back into the priming pan. But unless the match was withdrawn at the precise instant, the blast of the explosion was liable to blow off the lighted end of the match, so that the gunner was forced to bestow extraordinary trouble upon keeping his match alight. The flintlock was then invented. A small iron wheel was connected with a spring like that of a watch. This was wound up with a key, and held securely in position by a catch. A flint was attached to a movable *dog,* which communicated with a trigger in such a manner that by pulling it the flint was brought against the wheel at the instant the catch was lifted. The spring thus let loose, turned the wheel against the flint, and the sparks thus produced fell into the powder in the priming-pan below. The lock underwent various modifications, until it assumed the form of the common flint-lock, which is now almost wholly superseded by the percussion lock. As a monk was the first to suggest the application of gunpowder to warlike purposes, so it is not a little singular that the percussion lock, the greatest modern improvement upon small arms, was the invention of a clergyman.

CROSS-BOW.

We can not wonder that these imperfect small arms came into use far more slowly than did artillery. The last great siege in which the old catapulta and ballista were much used was that of Constantinople by the Turks in 1453. Gibbon, in his magnificent description of this siege, has not failed to avail himself of the conjunction of ancient and modern artillery. The union of cannon and battering rams, catapults and ballistæ, liquid fire and movable towers, distinguished this famous siege. But the long-bow was in the highest repute in England down to the time of Elizabeth; and upon the Continent the cross-bow was long held to be a more formidable weapon than the harquebuse. Even late as the reign of Charles I strenuous efforts were made to retain the bow as a weapon of war.

It is difficult to overrate the influence upon civilization exerted by the general introduction of the modern musket and pistol. The invention of printing has wrought a change hardly less notable. A few years ago, at an English coronation, when in accordance with old usage the Champion of England, clad in old armor, offers to do battle against the world in defense of the right of the new sovereign, it was gravely announced that the champion had at length succeeded in mounting his horse fully armed, almost without assistance. Yet the knight of old was obliged to train himself to vault into the saddle in just such armor. As such weapons and armor, and the skill to use them, must be confined to the few, arms became necessarily a profession. The knight of the middle ages, clad in steel armor, and mounted upon a steed almost as unassailable as himself, could ride over whole troops of yeomen and burghers, himself almost as safe the while as though he were entrenched in his rock-built castle. The soldier became from his position a tyrant. It was the reign of brute force. Fire-arms changed all this. They restored the natural equality of man. The robber knight, perched in fancied security in his stronghold upon some steep crag, found that it could be battered about his ears from the plain below. No smith could forge armor that would withstand the small leaden bullet. Any man who could compass the cost of a musket or a pistol even, granting him a quick eye, firm nerves, and a steady heart, was the equal of the trained soldier. Gunpowder is the great leveler. It alone has made democracy a thing physically possible.

The invention of the rifle was another great advance in the construction of the smaller firearms, though many years elapsed before it was generally applied to military purposes. The rifle, as every body knows, is distinguished from a smooth-bore by having a number of shallow grooves running down the bore. These grooves, instead of passing straight down, wind around like the threads of a screw, making nearly a complete turn in going the entire length of the barrel. To understand the effect of these grooves upon the action of the piece, we must glance at one or two points in the theory of projectiles.

If a musket-ball were exactly spherical, and of perfectly uniform density throughout, so that the matter should be equally distributed about the centre; and if, furthermore, it were fired from a barrel whose bore was perfectly

MODERN DEFENSIVE WARFARE.

straight, and accurately circular, of the exact size of the ball, so that it should touch equally in every part of its circumference, the ball would travel laterally in a perfectly straight line, which would be varied vertically only by the attraction of gravitation, which would draw it toward the earth. But no one of these conditions can be fulfilled. No such ball and no such barrel has been made or can be made. Let a musket be accurately pointed at the bull's-eye of a target; then let it be firmly screwed into a vice, and discharged a number of times. No two balls will strike in exactly the same spot. If the target were placed at the distance of a hundred yards, there would probably be a distance of two or three feet between the bullet-holes. The greater the distance of the target, the wider apart would the bullets strike. If the distance were a mile, the balls would strike some hundreds of yards apart. This deflection is owing to imperfections in the balls and the gun—imperfections which it is impossible to remedy in a piece with a smooth bore.

The object of rifling the barrel is to correct this defect. To illustrate the principle of this, we will take a common boy's top. If the matter of the top were equally distributed all around the spindle, the top would—theoretically, at least—stand upright when once fairly balanced upon the peg; for there would be nothing to cause it to fall one way rather than another. But no man ever did make a top at rest stand a minute, and no man ever can do so. Now, let a rapid rotary motion be given to the top, and it maintains its upright position. The same inequality exists as before; but by the rapid motion the heavier side is continually changing its position. The top tends to fall toward its heavier side; but this is simultaneously, as it were, on every side. The inequalities exactly balance each other, and the top does not fall.

Now to apply this principle to the rifle. The grooves wind around like a screw; the bullet fits tightly into them, and can no more be driven straight down into the barrel than a screw can be driven like a nail straight into a plank. It must descend in a spiral course. In emerging from the barrel it must follow a similar track. In a word, it must be screwed into and out of the barrel. The screw motion thus imparted to the ball continues after it leaves the barrel; and we may consider it a top spinning through the air peg foremost. All the tendencies to lateral motion being thus neutralized, it goes straight forward to its mark, influenced only by the attraction of gravitation, which draws it toward the earth. This being a uniform force, can easily be calculated, and proper allowance made for it.

Various expedients have been tried to make the rifle ball fit the bore. It has been made a trifle larger than the bore, down which it is forced by the ramrod and mallet. The American backwoodsman uses a patch of greased cloth around the ball; this requires less force to drive it down, and he dispenses with the mallet. Still, to force the ball spirally down the bore requires time, and rapid firing is of great importance in warfare.

The rifle, therefore, has never, until quite recently, been a favorite weapon in European warfare. It was introduced into the French armies during the Revolution; but was speedily abandoned. Perhaps the character of the soldiers of the republic had quite as much to do with this as the defects in the weapon. The ardent youths who flew to arms at the tidings of the invasion of their country by the combined forces of the Continent, had little of the cool calculating spirit which enables the Kentucky hunter to pick off the enemy man by man. The fierce charge, the fiery hand-to-hand conflict, the shock of masses, were more in accordance with their instincts.

After the occupation of Algiers, the French troops were brought in contact with a new foe. It was useless to charge against an enemy who would not stand the shock. The fleet steeds of the Arab warriors easily bore them beyond the reach of the French, while in retreating their long carbines told fearfully upon the pursuers. To cope successfully with these, a weapon was wanted which should combine the long effective range of the rifle with the facility in loading of the musket. Two general modes of constructing such a weapon suggested themselves: a rifle capable of quick loading at the muzzle, and one loading at the breech. Almost simultaneously kindred experiments were undertaken in Prussia, while the peculiar character of our own border warfare led to like efforts here. The result has been the production of three forms of rifles. The revolver in America, the *Zundnädelgewahr* in Prussia, and

THE FRENCH IN ALGERIA.

the Minié rifle in France. For close skirmishing like that which our borderers carry on with the savage, where a half dozen shots in a minute may be worth a thousand in an hour, nothing can equal Colt's revolver.

The Prussian *Zundnädelgewahr*, or "needle-firing gun," is a rifle loaded at the breech. The cartridge contains the ball and the powder, between which is placed a detonating material. It is discharged by forcing a thin steel needle through the powder, against the detonating material, which causes it to explode, the ignition thus taking place at the forward end of the cartridge, which possesses several advantages not necessary to be detailed. In rapidity of loading and discharge, the Prussian gun stands unrivaled; but its construction is so delicate that much doubt exists as to its efficiency in the rough usage of an actual campaign. If report speaks truly, after a few discharges it leaks fire to such an extent, through the joinings, that the soldiers can not discharge it from the shoulder. It is apprehended that, like the famous regiment of tall grenadiers of the first Prussian monarch, it is quite too fine to use.

In France attention was turned to perfecting the muzzle-loading rifle. The first considerable step was taken by M. Delavigne, who made the barrel of his rifle with a chambered breech. That is, the bottom of the barrel, where the powder was placed, was smaller than the bore above. The ball was of a size to pass freely down until stopped by the shoulders of the chamber, upon which it rested. Two or three smart taps with a heavy ramrod flattened out the ball, so that it filled the bore, and was pressed into the grooves. As a round ball would not merely flatten laterally, but become distorted by the blows, he used a conical one, with several grooves around it. It was found that not only was the force required to spread the ball lessened, and the friction diminished by thus reducing the rubbing surface, but the grooved ball traveled more truly, the atmosphere apparently acting upon the grooves as upon the feather of the arrow.

Colonel Thouvenin improved upon Delavigne's chambered breech by screwing a *tige* or steel pin into the breech of the ordinary rifle barrel. The ball passing down the barrel, rested upon the *tige,* around which the powder lay, exposing a larger surface, and thus igniting more rapidly. This rifle is the *carabine à tige* of the chasseurs de Vincennes.

Colonel Minié directed his attention to improving the ball. His ball is a leaden cone, shaped very nearly like a sugar loaf, of a size to pass readily down the bore of the rifle. In the bottom of the ball is a conical excavation, in which is placed an iron thimble of the same shape, only somewhat larger, so that it passes only part way up the excavation. This thimble acts like a wedge, and a blow upon it will drive it further into the cavity in the bullet, spreading the soft lead equally on every side. The first shock of the explosion, when the powder is ignited, of course strikes the iron wedge, driving it up into the lead, which expands and fills the barrel and its rifled grooves. The force of the powder performs the work of the blows of the ramrod in other rifles. The operation of loading consists merely in dropping the bullet down upon the powder. This combination of ball and gun constitutes the fatal Minié rifle.

Marvelous stories are told of the range and accuracy of this new weapon. A good marksman is sure of his man at a distance of more than one-third of a mile; at a distance twice as great the men and horses attached to a piece of artillery might be easily picked off one by one; at a mile and more the balls would tell fearfully upon a body of troops. At the battle of Inkermann, we are told that the Minié balls passed sheer through four men, killing the fifth. The most effective distance for grape and cannister shot is but three or four hundred yards—just half as far as the Minié rifle carries with perfect accuracy. A few riflemen, therefore, lying securely under cover might easily disable a battery. A hundred of these weapons well directed against Bragg's artillery might have changed the fate of the battle of Buena Vista. A troop of cavalry advancing to the charge would be for a mile under the direct fire of a body of riflemen. At Bomarsund and Sebastopol the French riflemen deliberately picked off the gunners at the embrasures of the Russian fortress. The Minié rifle must effect great changes in the art of war, by depriving the artillery of the pre-eminence it has so long held of being the most efficient arm of service. It behooves our own government to look to it that we are not found without having at command this new weapon.

WALL-PIECE—HARQUEBUSE—MINIE RIFLE, WITH SWORD BAYONET.

The present war in the East has given rise to almost innumerable suggestions and experiments for the purpose of improving every description of fire-arms. Among these is the "Lancaster gun," which is an apparently successful attempt to apply the principle of the rifle to cannon of the largest size. The chief peculiarity of this cannon is that the bore, instead of having grooves like the rifle, is smooth.

As a substitute for grooves, the bore, instead of being circular, has a form slightly elliptical, the major axis exceeding the minor about half an inch, in a piece of eight inches calibre. The longer axis, instead of running straight down the piece, makes a half-turn in its whole length. The annexed cut represents a section of the bore at the breech of the gun, the longer diameter lying horizontally. At the muzzle the longer diameter, as in the cut opposite, stands perpendicularly. The ball being of such a shape as to fit the bore, it of course makes a half-turn in passing from the breech to the muzzle, and thus acquires the rotary motion of the rifle bullet. The ball for the Lancaster gun is conical, like that used with the Minié rifle. Suppose an ordinary sugar loaf to be slightly compressed at the sides, and we have a perfect representation of this ball. The conical ball possesses two advantages over the spherical one. It receives less resistance from the atmosphere, and it admits of a heavier ball being fired from a cannon of a given calibre. It is the combination of the twisted spherical bore and the conical ball that constitutes the Lancaster gun. This gun has been put to the test at Sebastopol, where it is asserted that it has thrown a ball of 95 pounds weight more than four miles.

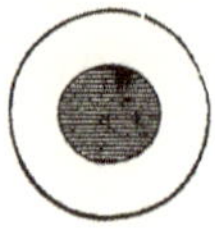

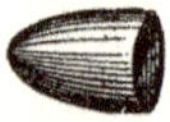

COACHWHIPBOOKS.COM (PRINT)
COACHWHIP.COM (EPUB)

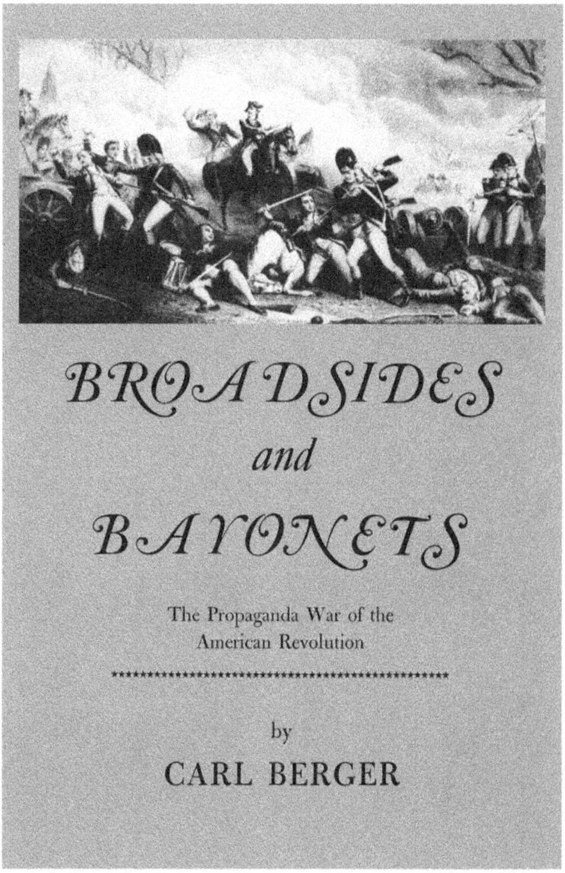

COACHWHIP PUBLICATIONS
ALSO AVAILABLE

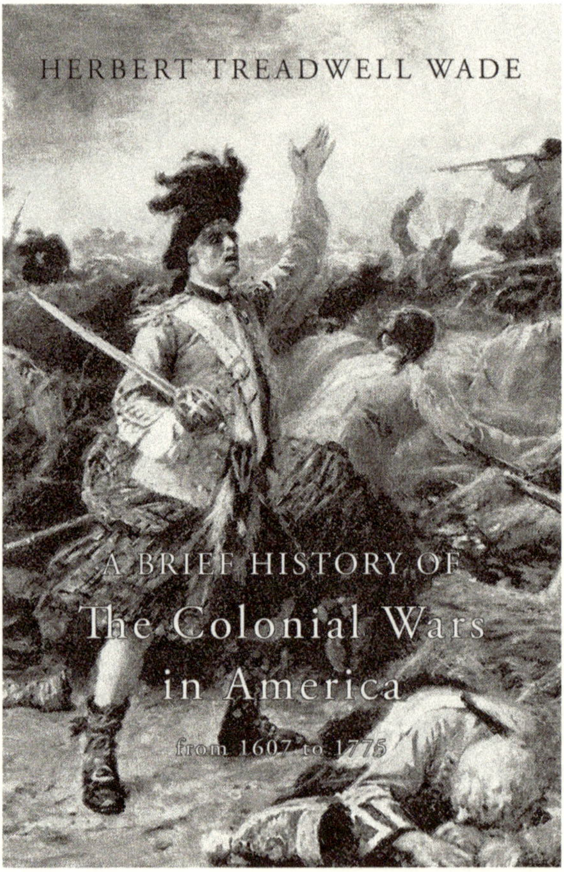

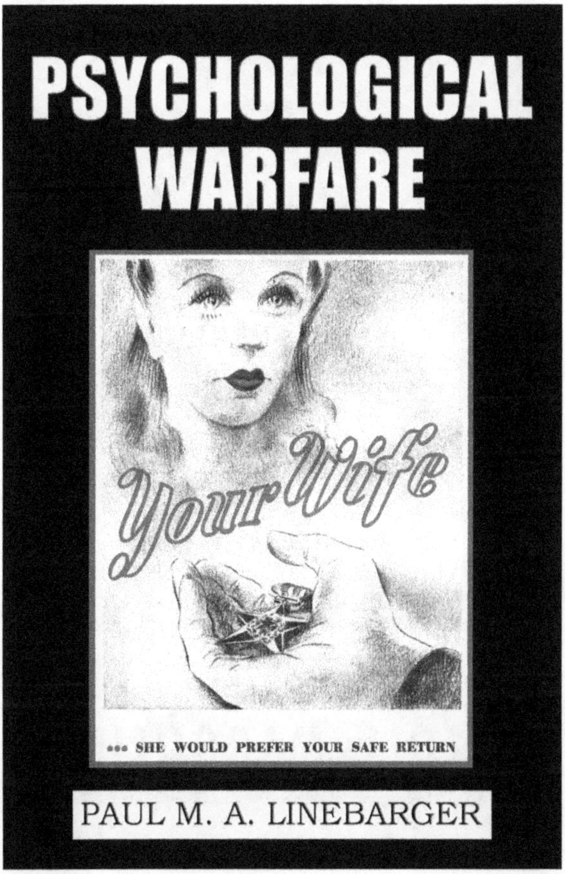
PSYCHOLOGICAL WARFARE
your Wife
... SHE WOULD PREFER YOUR SAFE RETURN
PAUL M. A. LINEBARGER

COACHWHIP PUBLICATIONS
ALSO AVAILABLE

FRIDAY, AUGUST 7, 1914
SPECIAL
WAR NEWS
STILL HOLDING OUT.
Against Onslaught of
PROPAGANDA TECHNIQUE IN THE WORLD WAR
HAROLD D. LASSWELL

COACHWHIP PUBLICATIONS
ALSO AVAILABLE

YORKTOWN
THE STRATEGY, PEOPLE, AND EVENTS SURROUNDING THE FINAL BATTLE IN THE AMERICAN WAR OF INDEPENDENCE

COACHWHIP PUBLICATIONS
ALSO AVAILABLE

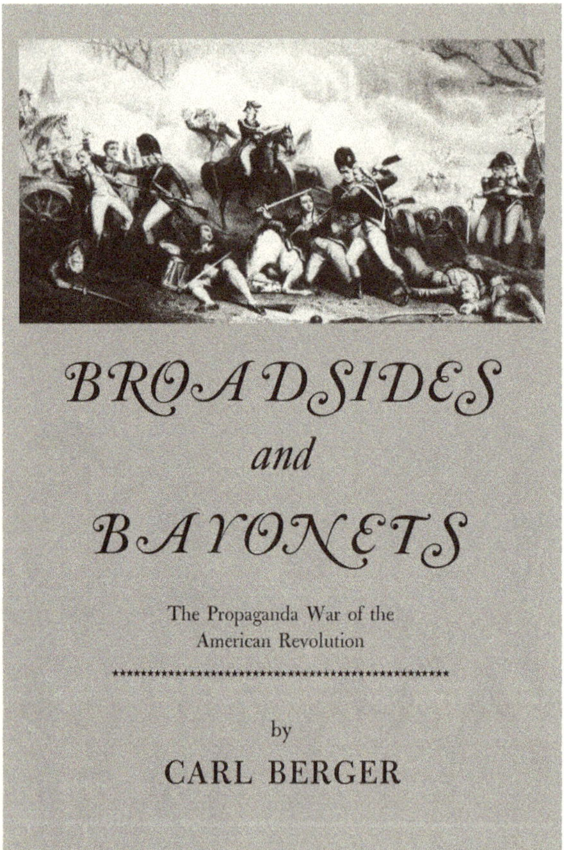

COACHWHIPBOOKS.COM (PRINT)
COACHWHIP.COM (EPUB)

www.ingramcontent.com/pod-product-compliance
Lightning Source LLC
Chambersburg PA
CBHW031946090426
42739CB00006B/104
* 9 7 8 1 6 1 6 4 6 5 4 1 4 *